Also by Mary Wyatt Byers is *Seasons of Life: Perspective*; Kingdom Publishing Group, Inc, Ashland, Virginia, 2009.

Reflections

Mary Wyatt Byers

WestBow®
PRESS
A DIVISION OF THOMAS NELSON
& ZONDERVAN

WestBow Press books may be ordered through booksellers or by contacting:

WestBow Press
A Division of Thomas Nelson & Zondervan
1663 Liberty Drive
Bloomington, IN 47403
www.westbowpress.com
1 (866) 928-1240

Because of the dynamic nature of the Internet, any web addresses or links contained in this book may have changed since publication and may no longer be valid. The views expressed in this work are solely those of the author and do not necessarily reflect the views of the publisher, and the publisher hereby disclaims any responsibility for them.

Any people depicted in stock imagery provided by Thinkstock are models, and such images are being used for illustrative purposes only. Certain stock imagery © Thinkstock.

ISBN: 978-1-4908-3908-0 (sc)
ISBN: 978-1-4908-3909-7 (e)

Library of Congress Control Number: 2014909986

Printed in the United States of America.

WestBow Press rev. date: 07/22/2014

Dedication

This book is dedicated to my family and friends who have encouraged me in my endeavor to complete this second poetry book. It is also dedicated to you, the reader, with the hope that you might be inspired to listen to God's voice during your own moments of reflection.

Contents

Acknowledgements

In thinking of whom to recognize for helping me write this book of poetry, I'd be speaking amiss if I did not give thanks first and foremost to God the Father for His extraordinary way of insisting that I pick up the pen and record what He wanted to speak through my emotions and experiences (usually very early morning). I'd also like to thank my Lord and Savior, Jesus, for always being there to mediate with the Father on my behalf during my doubtful and self-pitying moments. At times, it seems I could hear Him saying, "Don't worry, Father, she's still growing in her trust for what You can do in her life."

I would like to thank my sister Carolyn (who's very busy babysitting her first grandchild these days) for sharing her computer expertise in helping me transport photos for use in this book.

Finally, I'd like to thank my family, friends, co-workers and other individuals who bought copies of my first book, *Seasons of Life: Perspective* and their encouragement for me to complete another poetry book. I pray that this book will inspire each of them and individuals reading my poetry for the first time to have a closer relationship with God.

Introduction

As I write this, I am recovering from carotid artery surgery and watching Dr. Oz whose topic today is "Signs of Aging". Oh, wow! I really need that (sarcasm). The audience has just been quizzed on their facial skin by their responses to several questions about the lines around their mouths, between their eyes and whether or not their eyelids droop over their eyelashes. At the end of the quiz, they have been given either green or red cards that tell their "skin age" based on their responses. Green cards mean their skin is younger than their age, and red cards mean their skin is older than their age. I won't swear it, but I think that I would've received a green card (smile). Of course, some of us might've cheated just a little. At any rate, it's good to look younger than you actually are!

It has been two weeks to the day since my surgery. Although most of the swelling has gone away, it still bothers me to stretch my neck very far. I still have lots of trouble gargling, rolling my hair, and working at a computer for any great length of time, but I'm so thankful that it's not what it was a week ago.

Dr. Oz's show and my surgery have something in common… **reflection**. For purposes designed for the writing of this book, I'd like to give the following definitions for the word: *Reflection-* 1) consideration of some subject matter, idea, or purpose; and 2) an effect produced by an influence, such as a high crime rate is the reflection of an unstable society (Webster's Ninth Collegiate Dictionary, Merriam-Webster, 1988).

When Dr. Oz gave his audience the quiz, they had to take a moment to look into a mirror and then decide how to respond to each question (definition #1). I don't know about the people in the audience, but it caused me to reflect about how the years had changed my appearance and, if the truth is known, it hurt. One woman told how she wears makeup because it made her feel more like a diva. Obviously, she no longer liked the image that stared back at her from a mirror. Recovering from surgery has also made me reflect on what my neck looked like prior to surgery and how it now looks (definition #2). Regardless to whether we think it's important or not, we will be put into situations that will challenge us to reflect.

The Bible tells us that we, who are Believers, should be reflections of God's light in a world that's growing darker year by year. Jesus said that Believers are the "light" of the world and that they must not hide their light because others need to see the glory of God through the lives they live (Matthew 5: 14-16/paraphrased)

Cindy Hess Kasper, a frequent Our Daily Bread contributor, wrote "God has placed each of us in a specific environment that will best allow us to shine with His light." (ODB/10-6-2011) If we refuse to shine for God, then He cannot release His power in us to draw others to Him. We must not develop the I've-got-mine-and-you've-got-yours-to-get attitude.

The Apostle Paul said it this way, "But what things were gain to me, these I counted loss for Christ." (Philippians 3: 7). We should all take that attitude because God wants and needs us to be His servants. He desires all to be saved (I Timothy 2: 3, 4).

Reflection is not something we usually seek to do, but when put into situations that bring this about, we can be catapulted into a number of past happenings (some of which we'd even rather forget). It can be a good thing when we call to mind perhaps, growing up with family and friends with whom we felt safe, secure, and happy. It can promote sadness when we reflect on the memory of loved ones who've passed on into an eternal dwelling place while wishing they were still with us. Occasionally, it can even signal feelings of unrest or anxiety as in the case of individuals who've witnessed the untimely death of someone close to them. Have you ever reflected on some funny moments? You could be sitting at a meal by yourself or with other family members when someone says something that reminded you of something that happened in the past that might not have been funny then, but all of a sudden, you roar with laughter about the incident. Parents, especially mothers, often have the I-can't-believe-it periods of reflection. That is, when their children have all of a sudden gone from toddler to adolescent to teen to adulthood in, what seemed to have been, "the twinkling of an eye." Whatever the reason, we all have moments of reflection. Just remember that they do come, and they will come whether or not we expect or want them to.

Quite often, my reflection time requires solitude. Boy, lots of things can come to mind when we're alone! The poems in this book were wrought during my "alone" times and definitely inspired by God

Do you believe that God can speak to you through others… whether in prophecy or in general conversation? Over the last few years, I've experienced God's presence in my life in such ways. One such experience happened in January 2012 during a women's ministry (to which I belong) prayer and bible study meeting. Our leader, being led by the Holy Spirit, offered individual prayer for each person present speaking prophetically over each one. Needless to say, before she got to me, my knees were already knocking so loudly that I felt that everyone there could hear them. These were some of the words spoken to me, "Your hands are anointed. Write! You write about Me. Your writings will be for the healing of others."

Understand that I'm not telling you this to boast...definitely not! I share this with you because of something I'd spoken to myself in a self-pitying moment about a week prior to this meeting during my devotional time. I had emphatically told myself that I would begin writing only for myself because nobody cared about what I wrote, except me.

Well, as you can imagine, when that prayer was prayed through God's Spirit, what I'd said a week before was the first thing to hit my mind. Trust me, God knows everything we say or even think! So, for this reason, I present the poems that He has given me to share with you. I don't know who the "others" refer to, but I know that God does not lie. Therefore, I trust that they will speak to your heart and mind as they continue to do in in my own life.

Reflections of Family
(In Loving Memory)

During my moments of reflection, I come to periods of time that are rather difficult for me to reflect upon. Yet, without these special moments, this book would not be complete. These are the times when a song, a fragrance or aroma, or picture, or word, or whatever, can bring to remembrance those whom I have held dear to my heart and who now have crossed the barrier of time into eternity. I hesitate to include these reflections simply because I do not know whether some would consider them a bit too personal. Even as I type these words, my fingers seem somewhat reluctant. However, because it has been placed on my heart and in my mind to do so, I feel the need to include them. I hope that they will be a blessing to you and encourage you to reflect upon the joy of being a part of your own family.

Family is a very important aspect of anyone's life. God has given us family as a means of support and encouragement when life becomes difficult. Family serves as a means of identification and helps us recognize just who we are and what we should or could become in this life. With whom else can we truly identify on this earth, whether good or bad?

The first reflection is of my mother. It is the poem I wrote on the day of her passing on July 6, 2011. She and my father reared ten of us with love, care and discipline. She was 86 years old at the time of her passing. She was indeed the strength of our family and a woman of quiet faith. Although I cannot say that she ever voiced her love, not one of her children ever doubted the love she held in her heart for each of us.

Two of the reflections in this section are tributes to two brothers-in-law who passed away within months of each other (November 7, 2012 and January 15, 2013). They were both very instrumental in encouraging me to have my poetry published. They are greatly missed by our family.

Another reflection is of a first cousin's husband, named Johnie, who befriended the majority of people he met. He was an inspiration to so many individuals because of an illness that he refused to allow to conquer him despite the fact that he was left a double amputee. Months prior to his passing, he was partially run over by his own vehicle which left him with a punctured lung and cracked ribs; yet, he maintained a cheerful attitude. Johnie was also a good friend of my brother-in-law who passed away in January. They had both been truck drivers and could share many stories about road trips (if you had time to listen). His wife told me a few days prior to Johnie's passing that he had been greatly affected by my brother-in-law's death. Johnie passed away on January 29, 2013 but left behind a legacy of inspiration to many in the community, his family, and friends.

The last poem is not about a human being but a little dog who was much like family to us who knew him.

I trust that the reflections in this section will cause good memories to spring up about your own families.

I was inspired to write the following memory of my mother on the morning of her passing. I have not changed its introduction, but have chosen to leave it the way it was presented on the day of her funeral. My mother loved flowers, wild and otherwise. It was nothing for me to come to her house for a weekend stay and find small jars of wild flowers and those cut from her flower bed placed in different rooms in her house. However, one summer day I came and saw no wild flowers, only the cut ones. When asked why, she quickly replied, "Child, I noticed some tiny bugs on those things, so I threw them out!" Despite it all, my mother really loved the beauty of all flowers.

On the morning of my mother's passing, I looked out of my front window and noticed the colorful flowers that my husband had planted in early spring. This became the inspiration for the poem which I now dedicate to the memory of my mother.

Clara R. Wyatt
Photo courtesy of Ronald Bush

Courtesy of Carolyn Bush

For lo, the winter is past, the rain is over and gone.
The flowers appear on the earth; the time of singing has come,
And the song of the turtledove is heard in our
land. (Song of Solomon 2: 11, 12 NIV)

Give Me My Flowers

My mother loved flowers...any kind.

And that thought, as I look out my

window, now enters my mind.

I see in my mind's eye how she used to kneel

Shoveling the soil until she would feel

The readiness of it while putting in seeds

As perspiration from her forehead dripped like tiny beads.

My mother loved flowers...any old kind

And on bended knee you would always find

Her picking the prettiest... only the best

That had weathered storms and endured the test.

My mother loved flowers...many...each of its kind.

All arrayed in full color in rows fully lined

Just waiting to be picked by her cautious hand

Seemingly knowing life would be quite grand

'Cause my mother would care for them within this land.

My mother loved flowers...how do I know?

Because her face would show it...there'd be such a glow

Whenever flowers to her was given as a gift

It gave her such a spirit-filled lift.

She wasn't much with "thank you's" as she occasionally said,
But the thankfulness upon her face could be easily read.
Springtime was most probably her favorite season
Since blooms were plentiful and for that main reason
The few flowers in her yard and in the woods that grew
She'd bring inside with their varying hue.
Oh, my mother loved flowers as her children well knew,
And I'm so thankful she received many
before her life here was through
As I envision her now in Heaven's garden anew
Enjoying God's own flowers in full celestial view.

When Ronald and his twin brother, Donald, first married my two sisters, some of us family members referred to the two as "The Fly Guys". In fact, the memory of meeting the two for the first time is of the 'fros (afro hairdos), hats, shorts, and, at times, stylishly colored suits they'd wear. In time, the 'fros gradually gave way to shorter haircuts. It took a bit longer for the shorts and other styles to disappear, but when they did, they did.

Ronald was to later become an evangelist after a spiritual conversion that happened in his home one day during the summer of 1991 (August 12th to be exact). What happened at the time of his conversion will remain with God. Although Ronald shared most of what happened with his wife and a few others, our family, the church, and those who knew him prior to this conversion saw a completely changed Ronald. The "Fly Guy" title would no longer fit; and, thus, all who knew him began referring to him as "The Burning Bush". He could take one word from any conversation with him and turn it into a mini sermon. If you had the time to listen, you'd come out the better for having done so. He seemed to have been on a much higher spiritual plain than the rest of us. He, himself, once told me concerning his conversion, "Carolyn prayed that I'd return to church, but God put the church in me."

Ronald passed away quite suddenly after having prayed a powerful prayer during a bible study session at church, November 7, 2012, at 6:59 p.m. exactly twenty years to the date of his initial sermon (November 7, 1992). Needless to say, he will be greatly missed by his family, my family, and his church family, not to mention the countless other lives that he touched with his spontaneous sermons.

Ronald became an encourager and often displayed a non-judgmental attitude toward others, and could talk to you about what was bothering you although you did your best to conceal it from him.

One of the things he did for me was to encourage my poetry writing and to help me see the passion I had for doing so. It is, therefore, an honor for me to dedicate the following poem to his memory.

Courtesy of Carolyn Bush

"The Burning Bush"

Now Moses was tending the flock of Jethro his father-in-
law, the priest of Midian. And he led the flock to the back
of the desert, and came to Horeb, the mountain of God.
And the Angel of the Lord appeared to him in a flame of fire
from the midst of a bush. So he looked, and behold, the bush
was burning with fire, but the bush was not consumed.
(Exodus 3: 1, 2)

"The Burning Bush" glowed within our midst
Shining brightly, without one hitch.

Speaking words that could have come only from God
Wherever his footsteps chose to trod.
"The Burning Bush" for twenty years
Spoke encouragement to those with fears
Often putting their worries to flight
With words that served as God's guiding light.
"The Burning Bush" spoke words of praise
Throughout his converted latter days.
"The Burning Bush" never died out
And his Spirit-filled words contained never a doubt.
"The Burning Bush" maintained such a high flame
That his words illuminated without shame
The Gospel message of God's great love
Of which he spoke so freely of. (pause)

The flame has now been extinguished on this earth below

Yet, within each of us, the embers remain aglow

For "The Burning Bush" has touched us all

As he never faltered in his evangelistic call.

What can one say about Tack? If you knew him, you could say that he loved a good debate. If you met him for the first time at a social event, you could say that he was a conversationist. If you were a business acquaintance, you could say that he could argue a point (always in his favor). If you just happened to sit beside him wherever or whenever, you could say that he'd find out enough about you to tell the next person, making them believe he'd known you all his life. If you were a very young child, you could say that he loved to tease. Have you guessed yet the kind of person Tack must have been? Shy? Never! Quiet ? No way! Inquisitive? You figure that one out. If he believed in your ability to do something, he encouraged you until you used your gift or talent. I regret that he will not get to see my second book in print because, indeed, he was my greatest encourager/ supporter for my first book. One final word, if you knew Tack, as his wife, Eunice, has commented about him on several occasions since his passing. "Tack was committed to everything he set his mind to do." I presented the following memory of Tack on the day of his funeral.

Courtesy of Carolyn Bush

"Tack the Giant"

For only Og king of Bashan remained of the remnant
of the giants. Indeed his bedstead was an iron
bedstead…Nine cubits is its length and four cubits
its width, according to the standard cubit.
(Deuteronomy 3: 11 *New American Standard Bible*)

Webster defines <u>giant</u> as *a legendary manlike being of great stature and strength*. Although Tack was a relatively tall individual who was not lacking in weight or strength, I'd like to compare his character as opposed to his physical stature to being a giant in another sense of the word that means *to stand out.*

Tack was a *giant* of a man in his gentleness with children. He seemed to possess a great affection for the youngsters in our family and showed it by the way he'd pick them up, tickle them and then laugh harder than they would. I think the children never really saw his physical size but saw the size of his child-friendly ways. In particular, Tack loved his grandchildren. He shared a special love for Kendall and Chase because they stayed with him whenever necessary. He talked much about them in their absence; and, when present, they rarely left his view. In fact, I was reminded by my sister, Loretta, of a Sunday when Chase showed up unexpectedly with his dad at my mother's house. When Tack saw him, he was overcome with emotion and began to cry because he'd not seen him for quite some time.

Besides being a *giant* with children, Tack was also big in his beliefs. He loved a good argument especially when he felt that he was right. (Of course, that was all the time.) The family has listened to him debate with us about many things. Sometimes the conversation didn't even include him, but he'd jump right in to give us his opinion or to let us know what he believed about an issue.

Tack was a *giant* when it came to advice. Honestly, I cannot understand how someone could remember so much that he had read or heard. Tack could tell you how to eat a watermelon correctly with a knife and a fork or how to cure almost anything you had with home remedies (especially cider vinegar). Trust me, if you had a problem, Tack had the solution.

Tack was also a *giant* when it came to conversation. I used to wonder why Tack never stayed in the room with the men on Sundays at Pearl's house or whenever we had family get-togethers. I used to believe that he couldn't bear to part from Eunice, until the answer came to me a few days ago…Men don't talk enough when they get together and Tack loved to talk…about everything! Which of us can think of one subject that Tack couldn't speak on with, at least, some authority? Of all the things he talked about, he spoke frequently of his childhood days in Charles City. I'll put my bookmarker here because there's just not enough time to relate the things he would tell us.

Finally, there are two things on a personal note that I feel compelled to share. **The first thing**: Tack was a *giant* about encouraging me to publish. In July 1998, he purchased a copy of <u>How to Publish a Book and Sell a Million Copies</u> by Ted Nicholas and gave it to me. He was determined that I should publish. When I did publish (more than a decade later), he was one of my best supporters. I appreciated the confidence he had in my ability to write.

The second thing: Tack was a *giant* in making me feel like I was older than he. Every year when my birthday was celebrated, he would always grin and say something like, "Well, Mary, how does it feel to be getting older?" in a feeble attempt to let me know that I would always be a year older than himself. That would always cut deeply, and he knew it.

Well, Tack, guess what? You have now reached the place where you will never have to worry about age again. But even nicer than that will be that when I shall see you there, I won't have to hear that question, "Well, Mary, how does it feel to be getting older?" for all eternity. Until then, we shall all miss you, Tack!

**An afterthought: Listen carefully. Can you hear him advising Jesus on how to make the "pearly gates" shine even brighter? I'll bet that he suggested using cider vinegar. (smile)

*For further readings about biblical giants read:

Genesis 6: 1-4
Deuteronomy 2: 1-11
Deuteronomy 3: 1-11

To know Johnie was to love Johnie. As his wife, Evelyn, puts it, "Johnie was a people's person."

Courtesy of Carolyn Bush

Then He who sat on the throne said, "Behold, I make all things new." And He said to me, "Write, for these things are true and faithful." (Revelation 21: 5 NIV)

New

What can we say about Johnie......the man?
We could say that he lived and loved much within this land.
His family was first on his most favorite list,
As his grandchildren were always within his midst.
Johnie loved hosting cookouts for family or friend
That lasted well beyond the times they were expected to end.
He was also quite passionate about those whom he knew
And always, without question, he had a word for you.
Oh, it was seldom one of discontent uttered from his lips;

Rather, with words of encouragement he was always equipped
That was not only heard in the words he would say
But in his smile that shone as brightly as a sun's ray.

I've heard some tell Johnie that he had "nine lives"
Because he had been through much and
yet continued to strive. (pause)
With no sign of bitterness or unhappiness in his eyes,
Johnie... the man... was always ready to rise

Above the circumstances that came to make him weak
Of which none of us ever heard him
complain when he did speak.

One thing that he more than once spoke so proudly of
Were his "new legs" that he truly did love.
"Oh, I can do anything I want with these
legs," he boasted one Sunday.
Then gave us a brief demonstration to
prove what he'd just had to say.

Indeed those "new legs" enabled him to
once again drive his SUV truck
As he himself assured us that it was not just by luck.
To quote Johnie's words, "I'm blessed!"
Which being interpreted meant, "God is the best!"
Those "new legs" also brought him to
church school whenever he came

To reacquaint himself with Jesus of whom
he'd begun to speak without shame.

In Heaven, Johnie has received "new legs" once more
As I envision him walking…no running
through Heaven's golden door.
With a smile that only Johnie can smile
While greeting loved ones with each step and mile.
Only *these* "new legs" will never grow old and worn
But will remain "new" with each passing morn.

In memory of Johnie Grooms who *walked* among us with
encouragement and strength of character at a time when he could
have settled for just surviving.

The Wyatt and Ellis families lost a dear little pet dog during the summer of 2011. Although we seldom, if ever, heard Angus bark, we felt his presence whenever he was at family gatherings. He would walk daintily between people either seated or standing, as if a human member of the family. Every now and then, we'd sneak a piece of food to him when he'd look up at us with those pleading and lovable eyes knowing that Crystal (his owner and my niece) did not want us to. We shall miss Angus.

Angus the Westie

For every beast of the forest is Mine, and the cattle on a thousand hills. I know all the birds of the mountains, and the wild beasts of the field are Mine. (Psalm 50: 10, 11)

Angus the Westie was a friendly little pup
As I see him in my mind's eye with
"Granddad" Curtis holding him up
In his arms, carrying him from place to place
With a look of curiosity upon his hairy face.
Angus was a friendly pup, switching to and fro
Stopping here and there with a special kind of glow.

Angus did not always know what foods to sometimes eat
But would often stand patiently at many a guest's feet
Waiting for a morsel tossed…Wow! What a treat!
Until "Momma" Crystal came and would put an end to it.
But never did Angus once complain nor have a "doggy" fit.

Now that doesn't mean he always did his
best whenever he came around;
For it was told how "Granddad's" truck seat
was ripped while riding into town.
And "Grandma" Ret when asked whether Angus ever barked,
"Whenever he sees the cows," was her
swift and steadfast remark.

Angus did not take kindly to being all "duded" up
As "Momma" Crystal once learned while in a parade of pups.

Yes, Angus the Westie was full of life.
Needless to say, he knew no strife,
As he would readily hop into "Momma" Crystal's car
Waiting to be taken anywhere…whether near or far.
He would give a look of excitement and out of the window stare
As though saying to everyone, "I'm going
home!" with a doggy kind of flair.

Yes, Angus the Westie will be truly missed by everyone.
But, if there's a "doggy" heaven, I'm sure he's having fun.

Courtesy of Crystal M. Ellis, author of
Character Flaws and *How Sweet It Is*

Acrostic Reflections

Acrostic poems use letters (written vertically) for a particular subject or topic. Next to each letter, a word or statement is written horizontally which begins that letter to express something about your subject or topic. They can be fun to write, but, most assuredly, will give you something to reflect upon.

The days of our lives are seventy years; And if by reason of strength they are eighty years, Yet their boast is only labor and sorrow; For it is soon cut off, and we fly away...So teach us to number our days, That we may gain a heart of wisdom. (Psalm 90: 10, 12 NIV)

Time

Is fleeting and

Measurable but not

Eternal

The following acrostic poem came to mind after watching a DVD entitled "No More Tears" produced by Jan Crouch, co-founder of the Trinity Broadcasting Network. Jan had suffered for many months with depression. She was delivered from her depression as the result of having had a dream about Jesus sitting around a camp fire with His disciples and laughing about something one of them obviously had said. The laughter, as Jan put it, was so "infectious" that she awoke in laughter and her depression ceased thereafter. (Paul F. Crouch, Sr, *Hello World* Nashville, TN: Thomas Nelson Inc, 2003), 87- 88.

Anxiety in the heart of man causes depression, but a good word makes it glad. (Proverbs 12:25)

D arkness

E tching

P athetically and

R egressing

E ach day into

S olitary and

S ecluded

I nhibitions

O utside our

N ormal activities.

How do you feel when you have failed at those things in which you should've succeeded? Even more, how do others view you after you've failed? Dr. David Jeremiah, pastor of Shadow Mountain Church in California, during a sermon entitled, "Slaying the Giant of Failure" (February 22, 2012/Trinity Broadcasting Network), noted two important things we should remember about failure: 1) Failure is a fact of life, not a way of life. and 2) Failure often leads to success in our lives.

How often we seem to fail in this life! We, however, tend to view others' failures with a much greater disdain than our own. The following acrostic poem was born from this thought and Dr. Jeremiah's sermon.

*F*eeling increasingly

*A*nxious

*I*n a world that

*L*ooks at you without

*U*nderstanding the

*R*eal meaning of your

*E*xternal and internal challenges.

Try as I may, I still find it difficult remembering the "fruit of the Spirit" as outlined in Galatians 3: 22, 23. One morning around 5:30 a.m., I decided to put the "fruit" into an acrostic poem. It was worth the effort to have done so. Maybe you will agree.

Love one another with

Joy, so that we might live in

Peace, always being reminded that God is

Longsuffering toward us through His

Kindness,

Goodness and

Faithfulness, thereby teaching us to show

Gentleness and

Self-control toward each other.

**Okay, maybe the English scholars will question the punctuation, but I think we all get the message (smile).

Have you ever lost your courage to do something that you really believed you could do; or, what's worse, that you should've done? It probably has happened to us all at one time or another. It might've been during your school years when the teacher wanted you to recite a poem or sing a song in front of the class. It might've happened during a church program when you were called upon to say a prayer or be worship leader for the morning service. A man may lose courage when proposing to the woman he desires to marry. Whether you can believe it or not, anxiety is always with us in one form or another, even with some of our greatest world leaders.

I once heard the word **courage** defined this way by a radio evangelist, "Courage is fear that has said its prayers." (Adrian Rogers, "Love Worth Finding Ministry", August 5, 2011—Bible Broadcasting Network) Here's my definition:

Conditioning

Ourselves

Until we are

Really

Assured of

God's

Encouragement in our lives

We could all use peace in this life today. Daily we're faced with unexpected tragedies, varying circumstances, and uncomfortable situations. To complicate things even more, the news reports heard via television, radio, and other means of communication can take their toll on us. I am so thankful that God sends his loving peace to us whenever we are caught up in the midst of such confusion. Recently, I had to be reminded of his loving care and peace when everything seemed to be heading south rather than north. Have you had those kind of days, too? If the truth is known, we all have.

Therefore humble yourselves under the mighty hand of God, that He may exalt you in due time, casting all your cares upon Him, for He cares for you. (I Peter 5: 6, 7)

Positive

Edification

Amidst a

Calloused

Environment

Faith

(Hebrews 11:1)

Facing difficulties while

Acknowledging the omnipresent God

In all affairs

That may try to divert the

Heart away from our Creator

Grace

(2 Corinthians 12: 6-10)

God's unmerited favor

Resting upon

All of His

Children throughout

Eternity

Salvation

(Acts 2: 38-39)

Shed His blood

At Calvary that we might

Live

Victoriously with Him

Always, so

That

In His death

On the Cross we would

Never be found guilty of our sins.

Silly Reflections

Ever felt like just being silly? It's funny how you can think of the silliest things at the most unusual times. The following poem was born at one of those times. **Remember:** A merry heart makes a cheerful countenance, But by sorrow of the heart the spirit is broken…All the days of the afflicted are evil, But he who is of a merry heart has a continual **feast** (smile). (Proverbs 15: 13, 15)

Chips

A chip is not a chip

Without the dip.

Without the dip,

It has no zip!

A chip is not a chip

That has no dip.

Without the dip,

A chip isn't hip!

A chip is not a chip

That is not hip.

Without the dip,

A chip will never meet my lips !

Mothers are called on to do many things in the home. She is the cook, the cleaner, the doctor, the nurse, the dishwasher, the police, the mediator, the listener, and the adviser, to name a few duties. However, there are times when Momma just needs some rest, and God complies. Yet, even at those times, I wonder?!!

When Momma Gets Sick

(Proverbs 31: 15, 17, 25, 27, 28)

When Momma gets sick, she can't go to bed
'Cause there's dinner to be cooked and a family to be fed.
When Momma gets sick, she can't afford to stop
'Cause there are errands to run and floors to mop.
When Momma gets sick and just wants to sit down
Each of her children with her can be found
Asking for this and help with that;
Yet, she in a weakened condition is so unable to chat.
When Momma gets sick and just wants to be alone
Suddenly there's no one desirous of
answering the ringing phone.
When Momma gets sick and would love to close her eyes
Why does the family seek her advice…
to them she's now quite wise.
Yes, when Momma gets sick she can't sit around and mope
'Cause the family needs her love and care
and for that she just has to cope.

Oh, boy! Another one of my silly moments. Believe it or not, it's my way of remaining sane in a world that, at times, seems so confused. ...Okay, it's one of those days when laughter is better than tears! (smile)

The Body

(I Corinthians 12: 12-26)

Why is the body constructed so
That on each foot we have a big toe?
Why does a neck join the shoulders and head
Upon which lives hair that might be colored red?
Why are there knees between the legs and thighs?
I guess without them we could neither stoop nor rise.
Why are there two circles within each eye
Though neither can be seen whenever we cry?
Why are there five fingers on each hand?
But just try grasping things without
one of them within this land.
Why don't our heads turn completely around
Rather than only side to side or up and down?
Why don't we walk on our heads rather than our feet,
Or cross our eyes instead of our legs when taking a seat?
Why do our mouths shut with two "gates"?
Probably to stop the tongue from spitting out hate.
Why do our hands resemble our toes?
Now, that's one question I'm sure no one knows.

Can we pick things up with our feet?
Or stand on our hands to walk down a street?

Now, I realize this poem's rather silly and not very sweet,
But it will give you something to chat
about when you sit down to eat.

Computers! Who can live without them these days? Every household has at least one, whether tabletop, laptop, or one that can be carried with great ease, as an ipad. Some find it very difficult to get off them for any length of time...That's scary. But, what if...?

What If?

What if computers took command of this world

And began to control the people...men, women, boys and girls?

What if suddenly it all depended on beeps and blips

And none could utter one word from their lips?

What if everyone became computerized,

And the lights and sounds from the monitor hypnotized?

There'd be no such thing as quality time

And life would no longer seem so sublime.

If cursors our fingers and hands became,

We could no longer lift them to pray again!

What if our bodies were changed to modems,

And all we could do would be to load 'em

Connecting us here with someone there?

Our bodies would be stretched out everywhere!

What if our brains became the disk?

Now, for some of us that would be a risk!

Just think with my computer illiterate brain

I wouldn't have enough memory to get out of the rain!

What if our faces were a computer screen?

Some of us might never be seen,

'Cause there'd be trouble with our

modem…no memory…beware,

If we had to rely on some of our computer flair.

How many of us would just shut down

Searching for programs that could not be found?

No, I'd not like to become computerized

At least not if I'm the one to decide

Whether I'd rather remain as I am in this body of mine

Or be created anew with a computer design?

**Something to reflect on: Computers are undoubtedly one of the greatest inventions man has ever made. Today, they come in various forms from tabletop to cell phones and have the capability of doing almost anything we desire. Unfortunately, they seem to be consuming the attention of far too many. If not careful, this may cause us to spend too little time with God.

In the Book of Isaiah, the Lord had to remind the Israelites (His Chosen People) about who He was when they began to rely on things that had been made by them. Is He trying to do that with us today, also? Read it for yourself…*Isaiah 44: 6-20.*

Humans are warned all the time about over-eating. Of course there're many reasons why we need to listen to this warning. Weight gain is the primary reason since that could also lead to health issues like diabetes, circulatory problems, and the inability to move about as quickly and efficiently as one would like. What about animals? Should we be as concerned when it comes to them? Most assuredly so!

My daughter brought home an abandoned kitten more than five years ago that could actually fit comfortably in the palm of an adult-sized hand. It was a calico cat (female), and because of its color (orange, white and dark brown), she named it Yam. Last summer (2012), Yam was taken to the veterinarian for her routine checkup. She weighed twenty-two pounds! The veterinarian told my husband to wean her off of the dry snacks because of the fillers that are in them that were causing her to be weighty. He did, and for a while she was beginning to thin out just a little. However, a few months thereafter, he started buying her more dried snacks that were supposed to be "healthier" for her. To make a long story short, Yam appears to weigh just as much or even more now than before her vet visit.

Somewhat recently, I conversed about Yam with my sister, Loretta. I talked about her size, eating habits, and "bossy" behaviors with my husband. My sister thought the whole discussion was quite funny and suggested that I write a story entitled "Yam the Cat". I did not write a story, but managed to come up with the following poem and even found some scripture that might help us out, as well.

Yam the Cat

Then Jesus was led up by the Spirit into the wilderness to be tempted by the devil. And when He had fasted forty days and forty nights, afterward He was hungry. Now when the tempter came to Him, he said, "If You are the Son of God, command that these stones become bread." But He answered and said, "It is written, 'Man shall not live by bread alone, but by every word that proceeds from the mouth of God.' " (Matthew 4:1-4)
***Also read Proverbs 23: 19-21

Yam the Cat

Once thin…now fat.

Used to fit in the palm of one hand

Now so big she can hardly stand.

She walks with a wobble

That resembles a hobble.

She loves to eat

Especially kitty treats.

Much too big to walk upright on her paws

Though you may hear her coming…clicking her claws.

Yam the Cat eats from morning into the night,

Unless she's asleep…then the food's out of sight.

Is there any hope for Yam the Cat?

Or will she forever be too fat?

Each week my husband purchases food from a store,

But, it never seems enough, so he buys even more.

Each member of our family has suggested to him to stop,
Before Yam the Cat swells even more and just plain pop!
Sometimes we think that he's under her spell
Because she'll sit on the stair's landing and begin to yell
With loud meows to the top of her voice
And he'll come right down…having no choice
But to feed her once more
With another can of food he has purchased from the store.
Oh, Yam the Cat is quite heavy indeed!
Though my husband thinks not, it's all because of her greed.

Photo Courtesy of William W. Byers, Jr.
***Today, Yam weighs about 33 pounds (2014).

Heavenly Reflections

Believe it or not, some people have already been there and back through out-of-body experiences. Jesse Duplantis ("Jesse Duplantis Ministries" broadcast) and Todd Burpo (<u>Heaven is for Real</u>) are two such individuals. Testimonies about their experiences in Heaven prompted me to write the following poem

Heaven

(Revelation 21: 9-27; 22:1-5; John 14:1,2)

Perhaps I shall never experience a trip to Heaven before I die,
But I am sure that I will be taken there by and by.
I've heard its streets are truly paved with gold
And its inhabitants are youthful…they never grow old.
I've heard that there's some kind of
machine that takes you there,
And in a mega-second you'll be whisked through the air.
When the door to this machine puts you out,
All you'll be able to do is look about
And view the wonders of this heavenly place
Where people dwell of every race.
They no longer live selfishly as when on earthly land
But as obedient servants at our Lord's command.
There's fruit for our strength and leaves for healing
And everything's alive, even plants with feeling.

The attire for people seem to be a robe or gown,
But regardless to what they wear, all bow down

To Jesus who is Lord to all who's there,

And praise, praise, praise fills the air!

Colors of all hues that we've never seen

Are found in this place that's so magnificently clean.

Loved ones will greet you whom you might never have known.

Even babies lost long ago will be fully grown.

You'll meet Biblical patriarchs who were faithful to God's word.

All of renown, of whom on Earth we have heard.

Oh, there'll be so much in Heaven to see and to do!

But until then, I must keep working

until my life here is through.

Have you ever really took time to think about just how great and awesome God is? I can tell you from experience how humbling that thought is. We, as Christians, believe that He is the Creator of all things (the universe and everything in it). Who (in his right mind) would ever dare compare him-or herself to God? I dare say, however, that there are probably those who just might risk it (smile).

Only a Speck

(Isaiah 42: 5, 8)

Only a speck in this vast universe
Who's blessed by God rather than cursed.
Only a speck in this universe created by God
In which life so often is difficult…quite hard.
Only a speck in this universe so immense
Where things unfurl that sometimes makes little to no sense.
Only a speck in a universe so wide
Yet, an awesome God stands with me to love me with pride.
Only a speck in a universe without end
But an omnipresent God to my requests will attend.
Only a speck in a universe of darkness and light
In which God the Omnipotent puts all fears to flight.
To think that I'm only a speck doing my tiny, tiny part,
But God the Omnipresent lives within my heart.
Yes, I am only a speck in a universe so grand,
Yet the Creator of all things gently holds my hand.

Nick Vojarvich has appeared on the Trinity Broadcasting Network (TBN) on occasions and also on the "Hour of Power". He is a man of God who evangelizes throughout the world. If you get a chance to see him on television, it might surprise you that he has a condition that most people would consider to be handicapping... he was born without arms or legs. Yet, this man has been an extraordinary spokesman for Christ. The first time I saw him on TBN, I was captivated not by his appearance so much, rather by what he had to say. Here is one thing that he said that I was left with to ponder: "When I get to Heaven, Jesus will not talk about my physical condition, but will ask me, 'Who did you bring?' " He went on to say, "We are to be God's servants despite our limitations. He has planted within us gifts that enable us to win souls for Him." (TBN "Praise the Lord"/ June 28, 2010)

Who Did You Bring?

(John 4: 34-38)

When this life's over and we come to its end
When we draw our last breath...alone...without ne'er a friend
And we cross that imaginary golden tide
With nothing more than the single hope inside
That when we should reach that glorious shore
Our Lord and Savior will happily greet us before
Those wonderful magnificent gates of pearl
Where He awaits us all---man, woman, boy and girl
To welcome us to His Kingdom on High.

Don't let Him ask of you, "Why did you
come into My world totally alone
When the seeds on Earth had already been sown?"
"Why did you not pluck one from fields so white
With "harvest" so plentiful within your sight?"
"Did you not know you were called by Me to serve
Whether people were nice or simply got on your nerve?"

"Remember how I loved you in good times and bad
Though often you felt ne'er a friend you had?"
"Yes, I'm very glad to welcome you here,
But think of that "harvest" that once was so near
When those "seeds" were ripened...quite ready to be picked
Though they lay amongst "weeds" that
were dead...not "quick"."
So, let us look around at all who live on Earth
To find males and females who desire a new birth.
And when we arrive at God's beautiful heavenly gate
Jesus will welcome us with pride to His glorious estate!

It's been a while since I last made an entry in this book. Now it's time to reflect upon the reason this is true. Have you ever felt as though your private life was crashing to an astounding halt around you and you couldn't quite figure out why? After all, everything seemed to have been going fine, and then, "Wham! Bam!" All of a sudden you're moving at a phenomenal speed that is definitely not taking you upward, but spiraling downward. You feel as though Heaven has closed its windows and the Lord is no longer hearing you for whatever the reason. Without going into any details (since I know that we've all been there), the crash affected me temporarily in emotional and financial ways. God has been faithful, however, to keep His promise to watch over His children.

As everything continues to climb (with the exception of our paychecks), I frequently must pause and reflect on this truth: "My Father owns this entire universe!"

I Don't Have a Dime

Why are you in despair, O my soul? And why
have you become disturbed within me? (Psalm
42: 11, New American Standard Bible)

Let not your hearts be troubled; believe in God, believe also
in Me. In My Father's house are many dwelling places; if it
were not so, I would have told you; I go to prepare a place
for you. And If I go and prepare a place for you, I will come
again, and receive you to Myself; that where I am, there you
may be also. (John 14:1-3 New American Standard Bible)

I don't have a dime, but my Father owns all.

I don't have a dime, but my Father stands tall

Above every circumstance…whatever may befall.

I don't have a dime, but my Father holds all riches in His hand.

I don't have a dime, but my Father is creator of this earth's land.

I don't have a dime, but my Father made

the universe and all that now exists,

And He alone dwells above, within the circle of earth's midst.

I don't have a dime, but my Father owns the

cattle on every hill. (Psalm 50:10-12)

I don't have a dime, but it is my Father's will

That I shall one day live in His Kingdom

in a mansion, bright and fair

Where He will supply my every need

and of His riches I will share.

Do you really believe you'll get to heaven on someone else's good merits? Think again!

No Piggybacking!

Jesus said to him, "I am the way, the truth, and the life.
No one comes to the Father except through Me."
(John 14: 6)

There'll be no piggyback rides to Heaven, I'm sure
Because God searches each heart of the rich and the poor.
You cannot make it there on a mother's love
Or upon the wings of a mourning dove.
A father cannot help you to Heaven's gate
Though many times he's carried you despite your weight.
Your friends, though they'd love for you to tag along,
Could never take you with them…they're just not strong
Enough to carry you on their backs
Without stumbling and falling in their own tracks.
You cannot make it on a rich man's pay
Believing that upon him you can prey
On his money to show you the way.
Some think they can make it because they're good
And that God will allow them in just because He should.
But do not fool yourself by believing what men say,
Because Jesus has told us that He's the **_only_** way.

You must make that journey all alone
By living the way Christ has already shown
Us when He dwelt on Earth as a man
Teaching us to be obedient to God's command.
So, do not think you can piggyback on some other
As a baby in a papoose on its mother.
No, there's but one way to God's Kingdom above
And that's through the Son of His eternal love.

Who is like our God? From Genesis through Revelation, we get glimpses of God's great awesomeness. Indeed, He is everything that the Bible has said about Him...powerful, immutable, all-knowing, ever-present, loving, kind, compassionate, gentle, long suffering...just to name a few. Yet, in all His glory, these things merely touch the surface of who He really is! No pen can accurately write to describe Him. No human possesses the kind of knowledge to adequately relate who He is. We can only pinpoint His significance with our finite minds based on biblical teachings and our own experiences.

Isaiah 46: 5 says it all when God asks, "To whom will you liken Me, and make Me equal and compare Me, that we should be alike?" Then He answers His own question, "I am God, and there is **none** like Me."(Isaiah 46: 9)

Who is Like Our God?

O God, You have taught me from my youth and to this day I declare Your wondrous works...Also, Your righteousness, O God, is very high, You who have done great things; O God, who is like You?
(Psalm 71: 17, 19)

Who is like our God?

He reigns over the entire universe

Yet can be found in scriptural verse.

Who is like our God?

He upholds with a mighty hand

Yet speaks peace within any land.

Who is like our God?

He rides the lightning bolt in a storm

Yet has no shape of any form.

Who is like our God?

Never changing…immutable is He

Yet our past, present, and future, holds He…all three.

Who is like our God?

His voice resounds as a rushing, mighty force

Yet He speaks to us in a still small voice…

Who is like our God?

He has created all that we see

Yet is the invisible God in me.

Who is like our God?

He is the God of all possibilities

Yet takes the time to listen to our pleas.

Who is like our God?

He sends the roaring winds within rushing waves

Yet takes time to comfort mourners at many graves.

Who is like our God?

He is the Alpha and Omega…the First and Last

Yet He has no end and is eternity's past.

The Bible tells us that no man has seen God (John 6:45-46). How then do we know that He really exists? Perhaps we should believe the evolutionists who say that everything was evolved from something else. For instance, humans evolved from monkeys!? Maybe you believe in the "Big Bang" theory that says a giant nebulae exploded in our universe and all things came to be as they are. Now that should give you a real charge!

Well, the Bible tells us that, "In the beginning God created the heavens and the earth." (Genesis 1:1), that He made all living creatures "according to its kind" (Genesis 1: 24-25), and man in His own image (Genesis 1:26, 27). What do you believe?

Though I've Never Seen You

(Isaiah 42: 5,8: 43: 7, 10, 11)

Though I've never seen You, I know that You are there
Extending Your hand because You truly do care.
Extending Your mercy and manifold grace
Beyond Your boundaries to this earthly place.
Though I've never seen You, I feel Your presence
In all I do, I feel the essence
Of why You created me in Your divine plan
For the reason I now dwell within this earthly land.
Though I've never seen You nor looked upon Your face,
I know that You exist in an ever, eternal space
Where You are not confined by this life's time
But in Heaven's eternity which is sublime.

Though I've never really seen You, I know that You care
Because You have created everything---the land, sea and air.
You have given life to us all...
People, plants, and animals great and small.
Regardless to what any unbeliever will say,
You indeed are the great "I AM" each and every day.

Steven Davey ("Wisdom for the Heart"/Bible Broadcasting Network, 9/27/11) asked the question on his broadcast, "Is your body a temple or a toy?" In paraphrasing some significant points of comparison, Mr. Davey told his listeners that toys can be used until they become worn out then later laid aside and usually forgotten. He said that a temple displays the presence and power of God, and it glorifies Him. He finished by letting us know that if we have a submissive will, God can live through us. Now let me ask, "Which best describes your body?"

Toy or Temple?

(Romans 12: 1, 2: I Corinthians 3: 16, 17)

Is your body a temple or a well-used toy?
Can God place within you His eternal joy?
Is your body a toy, mangled and so old
That God would have trouble finding a
spot in it that's not grown cold?
Has your body (as a toy) been tossed about from place to place
And God can no longer use it to plant
salvation seeds in our human race?
Has your body been squeezed so tightly
then kissed and thrown away
And God can no longer use you to bend your knees to pray?
Then your body has been a toy which
has been worn and put aside
And God is unable any longer to be your one true guide.

Can God use your body to glorify His name
Rather than using it to give yourself some fame?
Is your will submissive in doing the things of God
Whereas, for most, this would be trying and too hard?
Are you being used of God to display His genuine love
The "Agape" kind that's unconditional
which is seldom spoken of?
If your body is a temple, it will be used of God
Though many times others may think you're acting rather odd.
When your body is a temple, it will never be dirty but clean
And the wisdom that you get will be insightfully keen.
If your body is a temple, God's presence you will feel
Since His Spirit dwells within it and
you've been eternally sealed.

So ask yourself the question, "Am I a temple or a toy?"
Can I be used of God for His everlasting joy?
Or, am I just wasting my time doing things that satisfy me
And not concerned about my life for all eternity?

Daily Reflections

Here's a prayer I wrote for myself. I pray it each morning as part of my daily devotion. Perhaps you'd like to pray it

Morning Prayer

For Thou art my rock and my fortress; For Thy
name's sake Thou wilt lead me and guide me.
(Psalm 31: 30)

Please, dear God, may You bless this day.

Guide my actions in all I do and say.

Give me ears that I may hear

Your gentle voice that's ever near

To instruct and lead me from morning 'til night

Giving me a calm assurance of what's wrong and right.

The following prayer I also wrote for myself, but I must admit, I'm not as faithful to say this one. I guess it could be that I'm usually pretty exhausted by bedtime and, therefore, tend to forget about it before shutting my eyes each night.

Evening Prayer

I considered my ways, and turned my feet to
Thy testimonies. (Psalm 119: 59)

I pray, dear God, that I've done my best
To represent Your Name as I now come to rest.
I hope it was Your hand that has guided me
Throughout this day, as I give thanks on bended knee.
I pray that I have encouraged someone along the way
Or aided a helpless person at least once in my walk today.
Did I greet a weary person with a warm and friendly smile
As I traveled life's highway with each passing mile?
Did I pause to see a stranger and lift his spirit up,
Or stop to give the beggar needful money in his cup?
Did I use my "sword" at all this day to lead the "lost" to You,
Or did that person leave without such
knowledge…without one clue?
I pray forgiveness for the things left undone,
And hope to do much better once a new day has begun.

Obey

(Acts 5: 25-29)

This is the Lord's day,
So get up and plan to obey
Because it is the Lord's way.
Come what may,
Our Lord desires us to obey
In everything we do and say
Each and every single day.
Nothing greater should outweigh
Those things the Lord puts in our way.
And in His path we ought to stay
Without a falter and ne'er a sway.

Why waste time worrying? It makes you tired but gets you nowhere. I know because I seem to always have something to worry about. If you are a mother, then you know what I'm talking about. Yet, there are scriptural references in both the Old and New Testaments that tell us to not worry. I'm glad they are there because I refer to them often.

Look at the birds of the air, for they neither sow nor reap nor gather into barns; yet your heavenly Father feeds them. Are you not of more value than they? (Matthew 6: 26)

Provision

(Matthew 6: 25-34)

The Lord God provides for us each and every day,
So let's be satisfied as He gives freely what He may.
Though it may seem quite small at times to us
Do not rant, rave, nor even fuss
For God knows what our needs should be
Before we even bow on bended knee.
Do not ask Him for that or this
For He knows when our prayers are simply amiss.
Therefore, the best thing to do is to say,
"Lord, what would you like for me to have today?"

And you'll most probably be pleasantly surprised
At all that He'll give you without having heard your cries.
So merely thank Him for all He's going to do,
And you will be more at ease when each day is through.

**Some scriptures about worry:

| I Peter 5:6, 7 | Psalm 62: 8 | Philippians 4: 6-8 |
| Psalm 55: 22 | Proverbs 3: 5, 6 | Proverbs 12: 25 |

While sitting in my car on Pantops Mountain in Charlottesville at a restaurant waiting for a waiter to bring my food order to me, some nearby trees that were blowing gently in the breeze caught my attention. A thought occurred to me, "Those trees seem to be praising God." Did you know that nature does praise God?

For you shall go out with joy, and be led out with peace; the mountains and the hills shall break forth into singing before you, and all the trees of the field shall clap their hands. (Isaiah 55: 12)

Leafy Praise

(Isaiah 14: 7-8; 55: 12- 13)

You ever wonder why trees lift their arms to the sky
Rather than hang them low to the ground that lingers nearby?
Could it be that to their Creator they're raising them in praise
To say, "Thanks for giving us life for so many days"?
When strong winds blow within the lands
They sway, then bow and clap their hands
Giving God the worship He alone deserves.
Then stand majestically erect as though to serve
Him in their own manner...their own special way
Lifting "leafy" hands as they appear to pray
Whether in the cold of winter or on a hot summer's day.

Which of you by worrying can add one cubit to his stature?…
Therefore, do not worry about tomorrow, for tomorrow will worry
about its own things. Sufficient for the day is its own trouble.
(Matthew 6: 27, 34)

But as for you, brethren, do not grow weary in doing good.
(2 Thessalonians 3: 13)

Anticipation

I do not know what a day may bring.
It may bring sadness or cause me to sing.
When I awake each morning anew,
My question should be, "Lord, what would You have me to do?"
Instead I so often find myself bound
With my own wants and desires as God must truly frown.
For this is not the purpose for which I am here;
Rather for Him to lead me whether far or near
To those who need a comforting word or so
Who may have lost a loved one and now feels low.
Or perhaps there's someone whose finances no longer remain
And is finding it difficult because of the strain.
Perhaps there's someone in need of a friend
And knows not Jesus who will love him to the end.
Is there someone to whom an unkind word has been said,
And his heart has been broken…his confidence shred?
Oh, there's so much in a day that God wants us to do
Rather than be consumed with only our needs in view.

Be watchful in all things; wherein, you might just discover a blessing!

Blessings

Blessed is everyone who fears the Lord, who
walks in His ways. (Psalm 128: 1)

Blessed are they who walk in His ways.

Blessed are they throughout their days.

Blessings he gives may not always be great

As in bronze, silver, or golden weight.

It may come as something as simple as

Being able to understand in a class.

Or it may be something thought of as small

Like a stumble that does not result in a fall.

Then there are blessings of great magnitude

That causes feelings to be put in a heavenly mood.

These blessings may come few and far between,

But nonetheless, they can be just as easily seen.

Apart from those tangible blessings we feel

There is a vast number of the same just as real.

Of which we most certainly may be unaware

Though they exist on land, in water, and in the air.

It's the beauty we see in nature that does abound

In the flowers we see and plants all around.

It's the melodies we hear in nature every day

Playing tunes in harmony on land or in a bay.

It's the beauty we see in a darkened night sky
With its stories to tell in constellations on high.
It's the rising of tides that we see and hear
As they cleanse our oceans without coming too near.
It's the sun that gives rise to each new day
Providing warmth to the Earth in its own special way.
It's the trees clapping their hands with much ease
Offering to us on hot days a cooling breeze.
Yes, God blesses us in so many ways.
So, unto Him, let's lift our voices in praise!

To my understanding, one of the lowest occupations in biblical times was that of a shepherd. Why, then, do you suppose, did the God of this universe, the supreme Creator of us all, would ever lower Himself to be compared to a shepherd?! Jesus, during His earthly ministry, told His Disciples that He was the Good Shepherd (John 10: 11-18.) When Jesus came to this earth as a Babe, His birth was first announced to a field of shepherds (Luke 2: 6-20). The prophet Moses had to learn the ways of a shepherd before God could use him (Exodus 2: 11-15; 3) to lead the Israelites out of Egyptian bondage. David began life as a shepherd boy, but when the Lord took him from the sheepfold, he became the beloved king of Israel. He also penned most of the psalms found in the Bible and gave us the most popular one of them all... the 23rd Psalm.

Here's my version of that Psalm:

The Lord Is... A Paraphrasing

Psalm 23

The Lord is my Shepherd, this I know.
He's my constant Companion in this world below.
He maketh me to lie down in pastures of green
And watches over me when circumstances are not as they seem.
He leadeth me by the waters so still
Giving me peacefulness of His own perfect will.
He my soul restoreth from thoughts of fear,
Quieting my anxieties that are oftentimes near.

My cup overfloweth with His blessings so good,
As He long ago promised His children it would.
And I, as other Believers, will one day dwell
In His presence forever... Won't it be swell?!!

Nightly Reflections

Outside My Bedroom Window

Job 9: 9; 38: 1-7, 31-33; Amos 5: 4-8

Outside my bedroom window stands a "hunter" in the sky
Who towers above all others… so regally and high.
His name is Orion, a constellation so bright
The name itself means "He who cometh forth as Light".
I awaken early to greet "him" in winter and in fall
While the others around "him" appear so contrite…really small
As his magnificence in stature and grace
Almost completely fills God's heavenly space.
He holds in his left hand a defeated lion's head
Which represents God's foe, Satan, so I've heard it said.
That ungodly "Lion" that seeks us to devour
Our souls for all eternity…each and every hour.
A fiery river issues from out of his feet
Representative of Satan's eternal defeat.
Orion wears a belt to which attached is a sword,
Suggesting to Believers that he represents our Lord.
His belt consists of three stars so radiantly bright
Symbolic of the kings who traveled to Bethlehem one night
To see the new King who'd be to all an eternal light.

Orion stands quite tall within the darkened sky
Illuminating hope to all through our Lord Jesus Christ on high.
He beckons to us, "Come!" as he has paved the way
To God's heavenly Kingdom where we shall dwell one day.

What is it about midnight that usually affects us in disturbing ways? Didn't Cinderella change from riches to rags and her beautiful horse-drawn carriage turn back into a huge pumpkin and a few squalid mice at midnight? Sorry, Cindy, but it happens to us all on occasions. We might go to bed feeling kind of good only to be awakened by haunting thoughts about things that may or may not happen just because of something in our past that caused us to behave in a way that compromised our good intentions. As Cinderella, it's usually a very personal thing that is only known by you and God or you and your "<u>God</u>mother" (smile).

Whatever the situation, it will eventually catch up with you... usually at midnight.

> When I remember You on my bed, I meditate on You in the night watches, because You have been my help, therefore in the shadow of Your wings I will rejoice. (Psalm 63: 6, 7)

Midnight

(Psalm 62:8)

In the midnight hours...the darkest of day
Haunting thoughts may try to come your way
Spreading their lies and being ever so near
Creating in you all kinds of fear.
They will tell you that God does not care
About what you're going through...your despair.

They'll toss accusations within the realm of your mind
Hoping they'll knock you down when they do find
Your weakest point that keeps you from the belief
That God hears your cry and will bring that relief
To comfort His child who's in utter dismay
About those mundane cares that now try to outweigh
The peacefulness God wants for you…without delay.
So, at such extreme moments in time
Know that God is there with love sublime

Just request of Him to tackle those taunts
To rid you of everything that now really haunts
Your mind, and in His omniscience give
You the confidence for which to live
A life more focused on what He has said
As you now find relaxation upon your bed.

Have you ever been in the company of a group of people, whether in a meeting or just so, and some are very opinionated; whereas, others seem not to be able to get a word in edgewise? Well, I am one of the latter people. For some reason, some folk can always get their points across in a conversation, etc. Do you think it's because they speak louder, or is it that they are better able to "cut others off"? (smile) Despite it all, there remains that voice inside of me that calls out, "I want to be heard too!" When it happens, watch out world!

> He who has knowledge spares his words, and a man of
> understanding is of a calm spirit. Even a fool is counted
> wise when he holds his peace; when he shuts his lips,
> he is considered perceptive. (Proverbs 17: 27, 28)

The "Me" Inside: The Saga Continues

(Proverbs 15: 1, 2,4; Proverbs 3: 5- 7; Ephesians 4: 29)

The "Me" inside cries to be free.
It's been held prisoner for so long,.,,,,an eternity.
The "Me" shouts wildly,
"Let "Me" out!"
"Until I relinquish all fear and doubt."
The "Me" inside gives a rant and a rave
Trying without success to behave.
The "Me" inside screams, "Hear my call!"
"I'm tired of being shut up within this wall!"
I need to get out of this pitfall below
So the world without will forever know

That I too have opinions of my own to share,

And if you don't agree, what do I care?!

I'm exhausted from listening to what others have to say

As though they have all the answers in every way. *(Pause)*

"Hey, wait! Joyce Meyers just came on…

Will wonders ever cease?!"

"Her subject tonight is on holding our peace."

"Let go of the anger", Joyce did say, "and leave it to God."

"He'll fight for us with His chastening rod."

"Lean not to your own understanding, my child."

"Ask God for guidance that's meek and mild."

"We must have a good attitude…be thankful in all

Because God's leading the way…listen to His call."

"So, stop allowing yourself to be upset over so much

And trust God to fight your battles with

His loving touch." *(Pause)*

At that, "Me" retreated and retired for the night.

Upon hearing that message, "Me" no longer seemed right.

Reflections of the Cross

I saw the film "The Passion of the Christ" for the first time last spring (2011). This was the first time I had been able to bring myself to watch the movie. My hat goes off to the actor who portrayed Jesus and to the producer of such a poignant portrayal of how it must have actually been on the night of Christ's arrest and the day of His Crucifixion. Throughout the movie are flashbacks depicting Jesus' life while growing up in His mother's and earthly father's home, times spent with the disciples, and special encounters with others.

The producer chose to include scenes that showed Mother Mary's desperate attempts to find Jesus prior to His Crucifixion. Finally, she and Jesus' beloved disciple (John) and another woman (perhaps Mary Magdalene) made their way to the foot of the Cross to watch her beloved Son die.

I'm So Glad

(John 19: 25-27)

I'm so glad Mother Mary was at the Cross that day
"Cause it must've meant so much to Him
as He hang there in dismay.
I'm so glad Mother Mary stood beside that bloody Cross
And watched the Son she'd raised and loved
though 'twas such a painful loss.
I'm so glad Mother Mary beheld her glorified Son
Though brokenhearted and helpless, she
understood what must be done.

I'm so glad Mother Mary came to behold
the Son whom she did love
I'm sure it must have pleased Father God
from His dwelling high above.
I'm so glad Mother Mary stood beneath that bloodstained tree
While the Son she'd beheld hang dying for you and me.
I'm so glad Mother Mary stayed from
the sixth to that very last hour
When with one final breath He committed
to the Father all His glorious power.

I'm so glad Mother Mary came to be by Jesus' side
To be a witness to the world that her Son had truly died.
I'm so glad Mother Mary held in her arms once more
God's only begotten Son whom she long ago once bore
When taken from off the Cross in the solemnity of that day
Though most had completely forsaken
Him and gone their separate way.

The following poem was also borne from watching the movie, "The Passion of the Christ". What an awe-inspiring movie! If you can watch that movie without shedding a tear or being renewed in the faith, then you must be one of Satan's offspring.

What More Can He Do?

(Daniel 7: 13-27)

What more can He do?
He suffered, bled, and died for me and you.
He took the weight of our sins to the Cross
To make sure our souls would not be forever lost.
He stayed there for hours in pure agony
As many jeered and mocked Him as He hang upon that tree.
He took much spittle upon His face
After being arrested for the human race.
The insults and disbelief He, too, did bear;
Yet, throughout it all He continued to care.
He kept His focus on why He had come
To obey His Father and to increase His Kingdom.
What more can He do for this undeserving race?
He no more will die in this mundane place.
But He will return as the Bible has taught
To conquer Satan in a final battle that's fought.
And peace will forever reign upon this earth
As Believers everywhere will experience a new birth.

Have you ever wondered about how God the Father must have felt on the day of the Crucifixion? I have. I realize that it was He who sent His Son to die for our sins, but I cannot help believing that if God has the same kind of emotions as He has given us, then He, too, had to have been quite affected by the things that His Only Begotten Son encountered leading up to and on the day of Jesus's crucifixion. Here's what I imagined that might've happened in Heaven.

When God Held Back His Power

(John Chapters 18-19; Matthew 26: 47-27: 54;
Mark 14: 43-15: 39; Luke 22: 47-23:47)

When God held back His power at the time of Jesus's arrest,

He quietly closed His window as Jesus endured "the test".

Oh, He knew what was happening to His one and only Son

But refused to offer Him assistance once "the test" had begun.

As Jesus was led from "the Garden"

hands bound with some rope,

His disciples fled far away upon losing all their hope.

When Jesus was brought before the Chief

Priests and accusations hurled

God silently listened in Heaven as their untruths were unfurled.

When Jesus was taken to Pontius Pilate

and before him had to stand,

God quietly waited for His Son to

continue with His salvation plan.

When Pilate sent Him to Herod, being the ruler of Galilee,
Herod was quite disappointed for no miracles did he see.
And God sat unmoved though Herod's men
of war taunted with much glee.
When the soldiers plaited a thorny crown
upon Jesus's glorious head
And whipped and spat upon Him until He was nearly dead,
God remained quite quiet in Heaven refusing again to look
Upon what His Son was going through though
His heart must really have shook.
Jesus, then being led to Calvary along that old rocky road
Too weary…too tired…too weak to bear
that shameful heavy load.
Though God still stayed in Heaven, He'd
prepared someone to help along the way
As the weight of the cross upon Him
caused His legs to bend and sway.
God heard those soldiers pound the nails into
the feet and hands of His dear Son
But still He remained in Heaven, seemingly
unshaken by what was being done.
As Jesus hang there dying amongst the
shouts of those who jeered,
God's great heart was broken with a
darkness that everyone feared.
Then Jesus spoke with a voice that was loud and, oh, so clear,
"It is finished!" And all who'd gathered
that day, most certainly did hear.

Then God unleashed His power and uprooted the earth around
While the temple's veil was shaken and torn completely down.
Graves were opened…the saints released,
and into the city they did trod
As the centurion praised our Savior saying,
"Truly this was the Son of God!"

Considering all that Christ Jesus went through while here on Earth during His ministry and especially throughout the hours of His arrest, trial, and Crucifixion, I give Him the praise and honor that can only be bestowed on Him. No human being could have orchestrated such an awesome plan of Salvation. Only God Almighty Himself could secure our souls from an eternal death. If I had a thousand tongues (as the expression goes), I could never thank Him enough for what He has done for us all.

Truth

Pilate therefore said to Him, "So You are a King?" Jesus answered, "You say correctly that I am a King. For this I have been born, and for this I have come into the world, to bear witness to the truth. Everyone who is of the truth hears My voice." Pilate said to Him, "What is truth?" And when he had said this, he went out again to the Jews, and said to them, "I find no guilt in Him." (John 18: 37-38, <u>New American Standard Bible</u>) (Also read Isaiah 53)

He took our stripes to set us free,

And, in so doing, gave us eternity.

He took our shame upon His head,

And, in so doing, conquered the dead.

He took the spital upon His face,

And, in so doing, displayed God's grace.

He wore the thorny crown pressed upon His brow,

And, in so doing, showed us that He'd kept His vow.

He took the lashes across His back,

And, in so doing, He offered no slack

To what He had come to do
In obedience to God His Father, for me and you.
He took the nails in His hands and feet,
And, in so doing, Death He did defeat.
Yes, He did all this for me and you
To let us know God's love was true.

Many have speculated and aggravated over who Jesus is/was? Some believe Him to have been just another great prophet. Some have said that He was just a person who could heal. Then there are those who say that He never really existed, only make-believe. Perhaps you still wrestle with knowing more about Him. Jesus Himself has already defined who He is and why He was born in the Gospels (Matthew, Mark, Luke, & John). Although the first three Gospel writers do much to show the teachings and healings of Jesus, it is the book of John that pinpoints exactly who Jesus is. Why? Because Jesus Himself testifies of Himself. Read it for yourself. A good place to begin is John 14: 6.

When Jesus came into the region of Caesarea, Philippi, He asked His disciples, saying, "Who do men say that I, the Son of Man, am?" So they said, "Some say John the Baptist, some Elijah, and others Jermiah or one of the prophets." He said to them, "But who do you say that I am?" (Matthew 16:13-15)

Who Do You Say I Am?

Mark 8:27-9:1; Matthew 16:13-19
John chapters 14, 15, 16, & 17

Elijah or John the Baptist, some have called Me,
But I am neither of them as You will see.
I Am the Messiah…the Christ of all on Earth
Who is willing to receive a spiritual birth.
I came to set each one apart
And to give them a new and loving heart.

I came to teach about My Father's home
Wherever I so choose to roam.
I came to set the record straight
That **I Am** the <u>only</u> way to Heaven's gate.
I came that you might have life more abundantly
That's why I chose to die for your sins upon a rugged tree.
I came and humbled myself as a man
That I might feel your sorrows within this land.
I came willingly at My Father's command
For He **so** loved you with an outstretched hand.
Now, to answer the question about who **I Am**,
I Am the ultimate sacrificial Lamb
Who gave His life that you might live, not die
But receive eternal life beyond the sky.

Miscellaneous Reflections

For thirty-one years (Yes, 31 years!), I was a Special Educator. When I tell you that there was never a dull moment during my years of teaching, I mean it literally! The poem below was the result of one very stressful year of teaching. You'll see what I mean. Of course, the names have been changed, but not the incidents. (smile)

School Year _____?

(Romans 8: 28; I Peter 5: 6- 7,10-11)

Let's see, the school year started out not so very good
Because of a child in my room whose last name was Hood.
He cursed and cajoled using all kinds of ugly words
Belittling others to shame with phrases
most people had never heard
But thanks to You, dear Lord, above
That when I thought You'd forgotten,
You sent your merciful love
And had this child removed from out of my special class.
You knew I felt like leaping and shouting, "Yes!!! At last!!!"
But under certain circumstances (You know the kind I mean.)
I had to remain cool, calm, and collected
without making a scene.

Unfortunately for me, he was only one of two.
And once he left, the second had quite a hullabaloo!
In many ways this child was far worse than the first.
To put it mildly, he was the worst of the worst!!!

He did things such as threatening others
with verbal and physical abuse.
No classroom was to contain him 'cause
somehow he'd always get loose
And go outside to block the doorway
Regardless of what anyone would say.
The assistant principal even came to try and move him away,
But finally gave up the struggle when he too was held at bay.
"I felt like a Sumo wrestler," he later to me once said.,
'Cause both he and the child were weighty…
from the toes up to the head.
We secretly tried to record him on one cassette…or two,
But he himself would turn it on until the thing was through!
He once dared to hold a basketball high, above my head
As I sat there fearfully thinking, "I know I'm as good as dead."
But for some unknown reason (I'm unsure of which one.)
He slowly walked away…I guess he'd had his fun.

Anyway, this child too was taken from my nest.
Then I knew without a doubt how God does truly bless
Those of us who are the called, according to His will
When He saw beyond a doubt that I had had my fill!!!

Small wonder I've paused to count my blessings at this time
Because I'm truly thankful that I'm still of sound mind!

God has, by His Holy Spirit, given us gifts that we may use to glorify His name and whereby we can earn a living while here on earth (*Read I Corinthians 12: 3-11). Oftentimes, when these gifts are really put to use, we receive accolades (expressions of praise) from our earthly counterparts (other people). If we forget to thank God for His blessings of these gifts, I wonder how does He feel?

Accepting His Thanks

(Isaiah 42: 8; Psalms 136: 3,4)

Why does God allow us to accept the
thanks for all He freely gives?
I guess that I shall never fully know for as long as man yet lives.
Why does God allow mankind to take all of His praise?
I guess I shall never fully understand His extraordinary ways.
Why does God allow us to steal the credit for all He does?
I guess that it most certainly must be this way because
We are His eyes, His hands, His feet
And He would not have us to readily retreat
When others do not understand that the gifts we possess
Come directly from a loving God…though
this truth we seldom confess.
So what a great and awesome God that we most surely serve
To allow us to receive the immense credit He so truly deserves.

We all know them. People who, when times are toughest, plead with God to help them out of their present circumstances, promising Him that they'll go to church or accept Jesus as Lord and Savior of their lives if only God would make them well or help them out of an adverse situation. The trouble is, what happens after God has restored good health to them, or has made good out of a bad situation? God is patient and longsuffering because He desires to see all of us enter His eternal Kingdom. Remember, however, our God is not mocked, and we will reap what we sow whether now or later.

Winds of Adversity

(Galatians 5: 16-25)

I've heard many reports that You are not You
Though when life gets tough many believe it's true
That You are the omnipotent…the great I AM
And will come running to You as a speeding tram.
For a season of time they'll believe anew
As they pace to and fro, wondering what to do
About issues in life that have brought them low
And it seems they have no other place in which to go.
Oh, they praise You and lift Your name on high
When the winds of adversity cause them to cry.
But as soon as those winds have died completely down,
No longer can they on bended knees be found.
The promise they made about receiving the new birth
Is no longer remembered despite its worth.

But You, O God, are longsuffering I hear;

Therefore, these people may continue year after year

Thinking they're using You...the great I AM

Not realizing they're putting themselves in a jam.

Do they not know that You're giving them a chance

To inherit Your Kingdom whereby they must take a stance

About where they'd like to spend their eternity

Whether bound in Hell or in Heaven set free?

One day, I'm sure, they will all realize

That You have grown weary of their lies,

And they must make their final choice

Whether to believe in Jesus and whereby rejoice,

Or to continue making idle promises to just get by

Not understanding that they have a soul to save when they die.

While listening to the "Hour of Power" on the Trinity Broadcasting Network, a man who'd been cured of cancer testified about how God had answered his prayers for having terminated cancer in his body. We all realize that the Lord doesn't have to do one earthly thing for us, but isn't it great when He does?! I recently underwent surgery to remove a blockage from my carotid artery, and I, too, had many people praying for my recovery. God chose to honor our requests, and I am in the healing stage as I now write. Praise God!!!

I Believe in Prayer

(Philippians 4: 6)

Yes, I believe in prayer.

I *don't* care

If you don't believe,

But I believe in prayer.

The results of prayer is everywhere,

Whether you believe it or not.

I cannot fathom a world that does not believe in prayer.

Just look around at all you see…God truly does care!

Without a prayer, where would we be

Had Jesus not prayed in Gethsemane?

He might never have borne our sins upon that rugged tree

If angels had not been sent to Him at an hour when He

Needed them most, being in silent agony.

He could have lost all courage of dying for you and me.

What if those who were sick and at death's
door had refused to call on God's name?
In their hour of need, there might never have
been healing within their bodily frames.

Or, if those who've lost children both near and far
Had never known how to pray?
They'd be wondering still just where they are
Up to this present day.
Prayer gives hope and builds encouragement.
It gives us an opportunity to vent
Our frustrations and helplessness to a loving God
Who listens and responds, when times become quite hard.

Oh, I believe in prayer!
And if you don't, I really **do** care.

Washington, DC is one of the most beautiful cities in the United States. Beautiful marbled buildings and memorials of all kinds can be seen in this city, our nation's capital. I recently visited a few of these places in Washington with our church school group. Usually when we go on trips of more than an hour, we watch DVDs to pass the time. On this particular trip, we watched the movie "The Fighting Temptations" starring Cuba Gooding, Jr. and Beyonce Knowles. In the film, something said by one of the leading actors caught my attention and stuck. Although I'd heard another expression that had a similar meaning, I rather liked this one better, "When people rub you the wrong way, just think of them as sandpaper. In the end, you'll be all smooth and shiny, but they'll be worn out."

I Don't Understand

A brother offended is harder to win than a strong city,
And contentions are like the bars of a castle.
(Proverbs 18: 19)

I don't understand how people can be so mean.
Thinking they know it all as if they're really so keen!
I don't understand why some like to boast
Giving nobody honor, but of themselves they love to toast.
I don't understand why some make fun of others
Though we are all really kin...sisters and brothers.
I don't understand why some like to tease
Making no attempt ever to please.

It's no use trying to figure these people out
Although many times you'd love to yell or shout,
"Leave me alone! Go away! Just scram!
Because I was created by the Great I Am!"

The choices we make in life will either help or hurt us and, sometimes, those we love. Rarely do they remain neutral. If they do, the old adage that states, **"You'll always get what you've always got, if you always do what you've always done."** applies to you. One thing is for certain, we should never blame God for the undesirable circumstances in which we may find ourselves when bad choices are made. One of the best loved African-American singers, Whitney Houston, died yesterday. Whitney had a voice comparable to very few (if any). Yet, she made a choice years ago that most probably was the result of her early passing. Thank God that she had also made a right choice years earlier... to accept Jesus as her Lord and Savior. This poem was borne out of hearing about her death.

When Troubles Come

(I Peter 5: 6-11)

How dare you blame God for your troubles and strife
For God is a good God throughout our life!
If into deep pits we choose to fall,
God is the One on which we then should call.
Then why don't we praise Him before we're down
Instead of doing foolish things that causes us to drown
In a sea of confusion and heartache too
Rather than ask God for His advice on what we should do?
God is ever listening...He's always ever so near
Just waiting for our call...to lend a listening ear.

He's like a father wanting to teach His
children...old and the very small
Those things they need to do before
they're pressed against a wall.
All He asks is that we love Him and follow His command
And then we all will be blessed mightily in this earthly land.
But do not wait until your troubles, before
you praise His mighty name
For our God is not someone with whom
you can play some foolish game.
So be careful not to wait until your problems abound
Before from you, He's ever heard one single audible sound.
His heart is too loving for His children here on Earth
That's why He sent His Son to die, to give us a new birth.
But if you're so busy blaming Him for
the choices you have made,
Do not think that the Lord will come "flying" to your aid.
You must humble yourself and thank Him
for the wonderful things...each one,
Then give Him the opportunity to make
good out of the wrong you've done.

When trouble comes remember:

--We are governed by God's providence.
--We are growing by God's plan.
--We are graced by God's prayers.
--We are gladdened by God's presence. (Adrian Rogers, "Love Worth
Finding Ministry", Bible Broadcasting Network...5-26-2009)

God plants seeds within a Godly mother. She in turn plants these seeds within the earth. Just as different seeds produce varying kinds of plants, so does a Godly mother produce children of different personalities; and, each is a reflection of God's love.

Mother, God's Special Sower

(Psalm 127: 3; Proverbs 31: 16, 31)

Behold, children are a heritage from the Lord,
The fruit of the womb is a reward.
She considers a field and buys it; From
her profits she plants a vineyard.
Give her of the fruit of her hands, And let
her own works praise her in the gates.

A mother is the sower to whom God entrusts His human seeds.
She nurtures them with Godly love and tender care indeed.
She carefully tends her garden of many a varying hue
Making certain those seeds grow strong,
yet gentle, loving, and true.

The sunshine of her garden is the smile upon her face,
As she gazes tenderly upon it with the majesty of her grace.
Each plant that grows within it is an expression of her love
Showered daily with God's rain…sprinkled from above.
Often they bend and sway beneath the storms of life,
But a mother is always there with
encouragement through each strife.

As are the many colors in an earthly garden, all grown,

So are the uniqueness of a mother's children

in the home she calls her own.

To some, God gave the ability to lend a listening ear

As does the Godly mother throughout each passing year.

Some may possess the kindness that only a mother can give.

While others may possess her strength that

she endures as long as she may live.

Still others mimic her helpfulness in all ways that they can,

Just as mothers everywhere in many a different land.

Oh, the love with which a mother tends her

garden, surpasses the earthly kind!

For God foreknew what would be needful and

commissioned her as "sower" of all mankind.

Ever had a "pity-party"? Any one of us who's at least 20 years and older has. I can say that with surety. I've had some of my own and have known quite a few other persons (family members and friends) who've also "entertained" themselves at different points in their lives.

I watched my daughter, for far too long, engrossed in her own "pity-party" because of some things that had happened in her life that she viewed as defeat. Let me assure you that all bad things that happen to us may not be bad at all. Sometimes those "stumbling blocks" serve as "stepping stones" to the next level in our lives. The following poem was born out of my daughter's self-pity.

I Am Having a Party and You're Invited…NOT!!!

These things I have spoken to you, that in Me you may have peace. In the world you will have tribulation; but be of good cheer, I have overcome the world. (John 16: 33)

I had a pity-party one night.
No one was invited who was within my sight.
I complained about every thing that had me down
As I looked in the mirror with a scowl and a frown.
I asked the Lord, "Why must I feel so low
When everyone around me has smiles aglow?"
But He refused to respond to me with His omnipotent power
As I continued my ranting and self-pity in that hour.

Why does no one love me? Why don't they care?
Isn't there anyone with whom I can share
My problems with…my concerns and such,
Or do they no longer have that sympathetic touch?
Oh, me! Oh, my! I feel I'm going to cry
If nobody helps me by and by.

Just look at those around me…seemingly doing good
If their shoes I wore, I'd be as I should!

So, I continued the self-pitying and
complaining until my soul did groan
As I began realizing a truth that I'd always known.
The Lord will not speak until He's certain we'll hear
His still, small voice with a quiet listening ear.
He told me to stop the pitying and rely on Him
And not be so quick to give up though life looks kind of dim.
"Think of those blessings I've given you in the past."
"Why now do you desire to give up so fast?"
"Pitying yourself only serves to hurt
And will surely make you feel lower than dirt."
"So, get up, My child, I am still with you
Though difficulties now seem to be in full view."
"I will not leave you as I have promised to
As long as you remain faithful in all you do."
"Stop looking around at others you think are on high
For they too have problems, if not now, then by and by."

"Now, take down the decorations that
have caused you such gloom,
Clean up your act and with a new face be groomed!"
"No more pity-parties do I desire to see you throw
Because they only serve to stunt and not allow you to grow."

We all have seen them. Most home owners despise them. Some people eat them. Others make wine of them. Children love blowing on their seed balls. They can be used for medicinal purposes, supplying the body with many, many wonderful nutrients. I speak of none other than the dandelion (Old French for "lion's tooth" because of the shape of its leaf.)

I was asked to do a poem for a Women's Day program at my church. Now what does a dandelion have to do with women?" you may ask. Don't worry, I questioned God myself. However, it never cease to amaze me how God can use the simplest things in nature to teach us a lesson.

The Dandelion Within

She girds herself with strength, and makes her arms strong.
Strength and dignity are her clothing, and she smiles at the
future. (Proverbs 31: 17,25 *New American Standard Bible*))

While enroute to my sister's one Sunday past noon,
A dandelion I spied, that had perhaps developed all too soon.
For the dandelion had grown in such a gravel-filled abode
I wandered how it lasted as the many vehicles over it rode.
Yet, it stood with such a bright and colorful glow
That I stopped momentarily rather than continuing to go.
Indeed it had risen above a hard cold ground
And broken through gravel that had had it bound.
Then as I gazed upon that beautiful and fragile sight
I asked the Lord to show me how it related
to what I was asked to write.

The dandelion, as I have now found out
Is a hearty little flower that may anywhere sprout.
Godly women, just as the dandelion, are found here and there
Spreading their love in abundance as they so willingly do share.
The dandelion though amidst the rocks
still stood quite tall and straight.
Like that dandelion, women often must stand
beneath life's burdensome weight.

The trees on each side of the road had
fallen and long ago had died,
But the deep taproot of the dandelion caused
it to stand upright with pride.
Godly women are anchored with the source
of the Almighty God inside.
When the storms break forth in their lives, under
the shadow of His wings they abide.
The more fertile the soil, the more
abundant the dandelion grows.
The more grounded a woman is in God's Word,
the more productive a life she sows.
The heads of the dandelion consists of hundreds
of tiny ray flowers that're closely knit.
How often women are the key to joining their
family members so that each will lovingly fit.

The dandelion provides nutrients such as vitamins
B, C, D, E and P, to name just a few.
So, also, Godly women give of themselves
in everything they set forth to do.
When mixed with other flavors (as in a salad),
dandelion greens will improve their taste.
When Godly women come together, they encourage
each other in challenges they, too, may have faced.
Dandelions return year after year after year, despite
earthly conditions deep within the ground.
So, also, has God placed within women a strength
that in no other human is rarely ever found.
Though overshadowed by cloudy skies, attacked by strong
winds and bent beneath a pouring rain, the dandelion will stand
Anchored by its taproot, that lies unseen under
rocks and buried deep below the land.
So, too, do Godly women prevail, anchored
within by a God so omnipotent and grand.
Unseen is His Abiding Spirit within, holding
them lovingly with such a gentle hand.

We are so quick to point out the faults of others. Could it be that we enjoy making others appear less significant than ourselves? I wonder what would God have to say about us?

And why do you look at the speck in your brother's eye, but do not consider the plank in your own eye? (Matthew 7: 3)

Fault Finding

(Matthew 7: 1-5)

Finding fault in others is so easy to do
But when it comes to us, God asks, "What about you?"
"Do you see all the things that make Me feel blue
When you don't love others the way that I love you?"
"Daily you tell me the work you plan (for Me) to do,
But never quite "get around" to it. Now isn't this true?"
"Yet, My love for you remains completely the same
And though it hurts Me, of you, I'm never ashamed."
"So don't be too quick to judge others who
Never quite measure up, at least, according to you."
"You see, you now are in an earthly flesh
And quite frankly, it's kind of difficult to mesh
Among others daily without My loving grace."
"Just remember, they too are My creations in this human race."
"As I've looked beyond your faults to see your needs,
You must not shun others because of their deeds."

"For if we look past their actions and see each heart,
You will understand what I so eagerly want to impart
To you, as you live in this mundane life below
The seeds of love I desire for you to sow.

I awakened quite early this morning thinking about the goodness and everlasting mercy of our God. Here's the poem that came to my mind.

What Shall I Render?

Gracious is the Lord, and righteous; Yes, our God
is merciful. What shall I render to the Lord For all
His benefits toward me? (Psalm 116: 5, 12)

What shall I render unto You, dear God?

Shall I give You my difficulties when life is hard?

What shall I render to You, My King?

Shall I perform for You the songs that I sing?

What shall I render to You, the great I Am?

Shall I present to You all my worries that can overwhelm?

What shall I render to You, the Omnipotent One?

Shall I cast at Your feet my fears once the day is done?

What shall I render to You, my Savior and Lord?

Shall I return to You the love upon me which You have poured?

What shall I render to You…the First and the Last?

Shall I surrender my present, future and past?

What shall I render to You…the Bright and Morning Star?

Shall I submit to You the pain that I have suffered thus far?

What shall I render to You, the true God above?

Shall I bestow upon You a heart that's full of love?

What shall I render unto You, the Ancient of Days?

I shall offer unto You a multitude of praise!!!

One of my favorite animated shows of the past is "Charlie Brown". On one of the shows, Lucy Van Pelton (one of the characters) pretended to be a psychologist who (as the writer of the script wanted the viewer to realize) was only doing so for the money. Whenever a "client" dropped the charged amount into her cup before she would render her service, she'd always say excitedly, "I love the sound of cold, hard cash!"

Reflect on this for a minute or two......Money seems to be almost a thing of the past. Not too many people carry it with them these days. Debit/credit cards are now replacing many checks and money. Think about it, isn't it much easier to carry a small plastic card as opposed to bulky dollar bills and coins or a relatively thick check book in your pocket or pocketbook? Yet, how easy it is to buy more things because of debit/credit cards! It's almost a psychological thing... If you don't see your money being spent, there's less guilt about doing so. The only thing is that it's coming from somewhere, and guess where that "somewhere" is?! Perhaps Lucy Van Pelton had a point after all about loving to hear the sound of cold, hard cash.

The following poem was written at a time when I had begun relying too heavily on "the plastic". Hm-m-m, do you think that maybe I should have visited Lucy Van Pelton's office?

I Had It Out With Clout

Better is a little with the fear of the Lord, than
great treasure with trouble. (Proverbs 15: 16)
The rich rules over the poor, and the borrower
is servant to the lender. (Proverbs 22: 7)

"Clout," yelled I, "I've had just about enough

Of putting up with your kind of stuff!"

I can't even go into a store anymore

Unless there's someone there greeting me at the door

With, 'We accept Visa or Master Card,

Since we know that with most it's just very hard

To have cash on hand...Hey, look we understand.

After all, it's not your money...just the "plastic" we demand.'"

"Mary," responded Clout in his usual voice,

"That's not my problem when you make the wrong choice.

I simply relax in your wallet amongst your few bills

Silently and complacently, but it's your will.

Can't you control your spending when you go out?

Besides, you know what I'm all about."

"Clout," I rebounded anew,

"Just say the word and with you I'm through!"

"Now, Mary, that'd be too easy for me

Since I'm desired by many so frequently.

I don't want to lose my popularity...my good name.

So don't create such a fuss or my reputation won't remain."

"Clout, how many have you left defenseless and ashamed?

Or ruined their reputation...destroyed their fame?

How many have trusted in your plastic face,

Saying, 'I don't have the cash, but here's something in its place.'

How often have you left people wet in their tears,

Trying desperately to control their

spending throughout the years?"

"Well!" said Clout angrier now, "It is man

who created me...He set the snare!

And for that reason alone, I simply do not care!"

"Clout," I responded in a defeated note,

"It is true, this time, you've gotten my goat.

But the next time around when I speak with you,

I shall have but one thing to say, I bid you adieu!"

"Girl, I know what you should do!"... "Man, I told you what to do!"... "Wait a minute! If I were you, I'd..." Now hold on, "Girlfriend, I *know* what you need to do!" Sound familiar to anyone? Every now and then, I think about offering advice to others, and, on occasions, I have given it. The truth is many people don't really want advice, and would rather just have someone who'll listen to them instead. Some will take your problem and blow it so much "out of proportion" that you won't even recognize it. My advice (smile) is to pray and ask God to show you the best way to deal with your problem, and He will do just that...only be patient.

About Advice

Trust in the Lord with all your heart, and lean not on
your own understanding; in all your ways acknowledge
Him, and He will direct your paths. (Proverbs 3: 5,6)

When the ups in your life are suddenly your downs,

Please, do yourself a favor...don't go asking around

For that one word...that technical word, sometimes not so nice,

That word we all know... called advice.

It's something none of us really want to know;

Yet, it's amazing to see how quickly it can grow.

First, you take your problem to a friend

And before you know it the advice has no end.

He/she is suddenly an authority on what's good...what's bad.

While you're sitting there wishing you'd never had

Shared the problem with anyone...rather kept it inside
Because something so narrow has become quite wide.
"I'd do this," or "I'd do that," is the familiar phrase.
Knowing that if they followed it
themselves, they'd be half crazed.
Yet, many who give it have left *their* problems at home.
But it's guaranteed they'll always carry
yours with them as they roam

From one place to another throughout the land.
Now that *little* problem with which you began
Has stretched so wide that it's become quite *grand*.

Therefore, I've come to this conclusion as I travel along,
If no advice is given...you can't go wrong.

**Reflection Time

Thoughtful, kind, and helpful speech

It's a gift bestowed to each.

This the lesson we would teach:

Don't abuse it. (Anonymous) *Taken from <u>Our Daily Bread</u>, June, July, August 1990

Reflections of "Two"

Two Josephs

(**The first Joseph**/Matthew 1: 18-25)
(**The last Joseph**/John 19: 38-42)

Two Josephs were significant in the life of Jesus while on earth.
The one was at His burial…the other at His birth.
The Joseph at His birth took Him from His mother's womb.
The Joseph at His death laid Him in an empty tomb.
At birth, the one wrapped Him in some ragged swaddling cloth.
The other, at His death, placed Him in linen, pure and soft.
The first Joseph rejoiced for this heavenly King to see.
The last Joseph shed tears as he took His body from the tree.
The first Joseph received the gifts of
myrrh, frankincense, and gold
And must have stood in wonder as
Salvation's story began to unfold.
The last Joseph understood the purpose for each gift
As He helped embalm the King of Kings, the
frankincense and myrrh he sniffed.
The first Joseph taught his Son how
to build things out of wood.
The last Joseph learned from God's Son,
as sincere disciples should.
The first Joseph went before Jesus to Jerusalem's Passover Feast.
The last Joseph followed after Him up Calvary's
rocky path feeling like one of the least.

The first Joseph was full of God's Spirit being just and satisfied.
The last Joseph accepted God's Son and became fully justified.
The first Joseph died not knowing what
would become of his Son.
The last Joseph lived because he'd
believed on the Crucified One.

Humans are the same in so many ways. The normal person has two eyes, two ears, two feet with ten toes, two arms, two hands with ten fingers, two lips but one mouth, etc., etc. Yet, we are so uniquely different in personalities and abilities. God has created us this way. His Holy Spirit has also given us different gifts with which to glorify God. (I Corinth. 12).

If God has created man to be so uniquely different, what about the animals? There are many kinds of animals mentioned in the Bible...horses, donkeys, eagles, ants, grasshoppers, locusts, sheep, snakes, camels, dragons, cows, leopards...and the list goes on. However, there is one animal of which the Bible speaks in vivid contrast and detail. That animal is the lion. I pondered this contrast very early one morning (4: 14 a.m.) during my daily devotions, and the following poem was birthed.

Two Lions

(Genesis 49: 8-12; Revelation 5: 5; I Peter 5: 8,9)

There are two "lions" in this life
One brings peace...the other strife.
One rushes forward with mighty roars.
The other quietly seeks as He soars.
One captures to destroy his hopeless prey.
The other embraces to give hope along the way.
One is ever restless in his pursuit on earth.
The other is unchanging as He offers "new birth".

One silently crouches as an angry foe.

The other invites as He allows us to grow.

One has teeth that clench and stings.

The other has a body with protective wings.

One runs to and fro trying to criticize.

The other searches about to help make wise.

Yes, there are two "lions" in this life that we live.

One seeks to destroy...the other seeks to forgive.

We all get overanxious when it sometimes seems that God's time is not our time. Some of us may even try to help God along (Stupid, isn't it?) In the book of Isaiah, God Himself reminds us that His ways are not our ways (Isaiah 55: 8, 9). He also encourages us to wait on Him (Isaiah 40:31) regardless to how long it takes. When we don't, we most probably will get far less than He had planned for us.

Two Doors

Delight yourself also in the Lord, and He shall give you the desires of your heart. Commit your way to the Lord, trust also in Him, and He shall bring it to pass. (Psalm 37: 4,5)

Have you ever opened a door with expectation to find
Something that you're looking for...
just for your peace of mind?
There are two doors in our lives of which we must be aware
And before either is opened, proceed with the utmost of care.
One door is worldly gain which stands bright and so tall
Just waiting for you to open it at its beckoning and call.
This door, if you should open it, holds many enticing things
And is often entered by many...even
rulers, as Presidents and kings.
Behind this door lies great riches and even worldly fame
Frequently obtained dishonestly but often without much shame.
On its shelves within contain boxes in which can be found
All kinds of worldly pleasures that too readily abound.

If any of them you should open and inside take a peek
Beware to not dig further or you will
become spiritually quite weak.

The second door hangs securely on God's unchanging word
Behind it lies the many truths of which you may have heard.

It too contains many boxes on shelves upon which they sit
Filled with poetry, songs, history, science
and much prophetic wit.
If these boxes are opened because you've chosen to remain
Then you will find the Word of God that alleviates all pain.
For you will find peace, joy, patience, kindness and love
Given by God the Father and distributed from above.
His ways will not be yours as He responds to your request,
But you can be assured that He will always give His best.
So, which door will you now choose when waiting on God
During times of anxiousness...when life becomes too hard?
Will it be the door of this world with its fleeting pleasure?
Or the door of Godliness that holds everlasting treasure?

Reflections of Encouragement

Sometimes life can bring you to your knees. When it does, encourage yourself in the Lord. Quite unexpectedly, a powerful force of anxiety almost conquered me one day in mid-June (2012). Do not underestimate Satan's powers, but thank God that He can protect us against any opposing spirit that may seek to attack His children. Did not the Apostle John say, "Greater is He who's in you than he who is in the world"? (I John 4:4) Believe it because it's true. This poem was written in the midst of my depression that same day.

Finally, my brethren, be strong in the Lord and in the power
of His might... For we do not wrestle against flesh and
blood, but against principalities, against powers, against
the rulers of the darkness of this age, against spiritual hosts
of wickedness in high places. (Ephesians 6: 10, 12)

Encourage Yourself in the Lord

Isaiah 41: 10, 13; Ephesians 6: 10-13

They say I'm strong.
I say they're wrong.
They say I'm unique.
I tell them I'm weak.
They say you're wrong.
I declare that I'm not strong!
They think I'm God's child.
Yet, all the while
I seem to be drowning
And I cannot cease from frowning.

They believe I'm God-sent.
I say my soul is rent,
And for that I must repent.

I ask, "Will God receive my broken heart
That I gave Him from the start?"
God answers, "Yes, My child, for you I've always known
And the many seeds you've already sown."
"When, dear Lord, did I sow these seeds?"
"Whenever some person had a need."
"It was in that smile you gave to another
Whether a mother, father, sister or brother."
"'Twas in that encouraging word
Given to someone depressed that was heard
From your lips when she was cast down,
Who through your encouragement, I was found."
"Financial seeds also you have sown
That have helped others you have not known."
"You have served me in another way, My child,
By causing others to wear a smile
When they read the poetry you wrote of Me
That brought My Name honor and glory."
"No! No child of Mine is small or contrite.
I Myself will give him strength to win the fight
In this life on Earth below
That he will be equipped from head to toe
To battle the enemy that causes all woe."

Bless the Lord, O my soul, and forget not all His benefits. (Psalm 103: 2)

Wait on the Lord; be of good courage, and he shall strengthen your heart; wait, I say, on the Lord! (Psalm 27: 14)

Bless the Lord, O My Soul

Bless the Lord, O my soul!
Our God is awesome to behold!
He makes us well when we are sick.
He revives dead souls and makes them quick.
He lifts our spirits out of despair
Letting us know how much He does care.
He gives us wisdom to decide
What's best for us though driven and tried.
He puts our minds at perfect peace
Causing Satan's nagging to finally cease.
He awakens us after a restless night
Putting our wandering fears to flight.
He understands that we are only dirt
And how our minds can be so easily hurt.
Therefore, He continues to pave the way
And all that we need to do is pray
Recognizing Him as the only true God
When life's disappointments become increasingly hard.

He admonishes us to keep our eyes on Him
And do not things merely on a whim.
"Wait on God," the psalmist has said.
For He provides for us our daily bread.

Right now, I am listening to Victory FM radio out of Lynchburg, Virginia. The song that's playing is "I Know My Redeemer Lives". My eyes are suddenly filled with tears. Small wonder...I'm thinking about my daughter whom I have not seen nor heard from in over a month. As on so many occasions, especially when driving home from work and listening to the same station, I can actually hear my daughter's voice in a song. This is one of those occasions. My heart has become quite discouraged, and, as always, I pray, "Dear God, please continue to watch over and protect her, and, above all else, bring her back to Salvation." Then God reminds me (as always) "She's in My hands."

I don't know if there're other mothers out there who are experiencing a similar situation, but I'm certain that there are mothers who are going through some other pain or hurt. I hope that the following poem will bring relief to you, as well.

She's In My Hands

The eyes of the Lord are on the righteous, and His
ears are open to their cry. (Psalm 34: 15)
Have you not known? Have you not heard? The everlasting
God, the Lord, the Creator of the ends of the earth,
neither faints nor is weary...But those who wait on the
Lord shall renew their strength...(Isaiah 40: 28, 31)

"Regardless to how you feel today,"

(I seem to hear the Lord God say)

"Trust me, dear child, come what may.

I know your hurt, and I hear you pray

Though skies now appear to be eternally gray.

Just trust and wait for the one gone astray.

Do not to the right nor to the left sway

For My grace and mercy far outweigh

The weight that you now carry this very day.

Sometimes I work quickly and sometimes I delay,

But be assured, dear one, I've heard all you've had to say.

Again, I tell you, be patient with Me

though your skies seem gray

For I, the Lord, is unrestrained by time on any given day."

*Wait for the Lord; Be strong, and let your heart take courage; Yes, wait for the Lord. (Psalm 27: 14)

***Three days after this poem was written, my daughter returned home.

Now here's a sobering thought that we should consider at the end of any given day, "If it wasn't for God, we could do nothing!"(See Isaiah 40: 13-18) So why not give Him the praise for all He does for us on a moment by moment basis.

Let's Praise the Lord!

Oh, that men would give thanks to the Lord for His goodness, and
for His wonderful works to the children of men! (Psalm 107: 8)

Let's praise the Lord for all He's done!

Let's praise the Lord each and everyone!

Do not say, "He has never blessed me."

Just look around on all that you see.

He's given you a body that can stand, sit, and walk

And a voice that can be used to sing and talk.

He's given you eyes to see and ears to hear

Things far away or that are somewhat near.

He has put beauty in nature all around

Simply gaze at the mountain peaks or upon the ground

And see the beautiful flowers all in full array

Come to life in warm breezes as they bend and sway.

He's given us children to be our brood

Then supplied us with a shelter, clothing and food.

Look at the stars in the firmament above

In them can be seen a depiction of God's love.

Just watch them come together to tell the story of old
Of God's redemptive plan through Jesus is told.
Each constellation represents God's great power
And can be clearly seen in the night time hour.
Our God has given us gifts great and small
To be used for His glory for one and all.
Even the ocean with its praise does soar
As it rises so high and its waters roar.
The animals in nature never do worry
Because food is given them freely as they scamper and scurry.
Oh, our God deserves our praise in this life that we live
For it was He alone who of Himself did give
Us the gift of His eternal love
That we might dwell in His Kingdom above.

I recently watched an episode of *Andy Griffith* that featured Opie (Andy's young son) having to raise a nest of baby birds because he had accidentally killed their mother with a slingshot. When the time came for Opie to release the birds from the cage in which he'd nurtured them, it was quite difficult for him to do so. I began to compare the life of a parent when children grow up and venture outside the "nest" they once knew as home. Just as those young birds, they, too, "fly" away.

My daughter left home a few years ago. Although she's back, she still lives her own life. Most recently, our son left for academic studies at a university about 70 miles away. Our "nest" seems quite empty now. I realize that God is not only maturing my children, but is taking us (my husband and me) to another season in our own lives.

A Reason for a Season

There is an appointed time for everything. And
there is a time for every event under heaven.
(Ecclesiastes 3: 1, *New American Standard Bible*)

God gives us children for a reason
To raise them for Him in due season.
He may entrust us with many or just a few
Whatever the number, the responsibility belongs to me and you.
Then when it's time for them to leave our "nest",
We must say goodbye and believe we've done our best
In raising them right that they may "fly"
To their future endeavors set before
them in which they must try

And spread their wings beyond their "nests" of love
Though they may "swoop" occasionally when unsure of
The goals they've set for themselves to reach
Although we've been quite faithful to teach
Them about the ups and downs in life
That'll sometimes cause within them strife.
<u>But</u>, if they've been nurtured well and taught to stand,
They'll "soar" once more within this land.

Sometimes God must take away everything before we realize the importance of putting Him first in our lives that we might gain everything He has for us.

God Knows

(Psalm 116: 1-2)

God sees the tears that are in your eyes
He alone hears the true anguish of your cries.
The Lord knows the pain felt in your heart
And He'll be with you…He will never depart.
The Sovereign One knows your name.
Yes, you are the reason for which His Son came
To earth to die, that you might live
And in so doing He Himself did give
Up everything as He offered His only Begotten Son
Who gave up His life for everyone.
So, He knows the pain of losing all
And He understands your desperate call
But He wants you to know and realize
That His Son did not stay buried but He did rise.
And just as He rose in newness of life you too shall see
How the Lord our God will also set you free
From things that may bound you, keeping you down
Causing you to worry and to wear a frown.
Indeed just remember that our God knows all
Whether your problem is great or really quite small.

Life deals us some terrible blows from time to time. Someone has said, "When life gives me lemons, I make lemonade." How do you respond?

Praise Him Anyway

Every day I will bless You, and I will praise Your
name forever and ever. (Psalm 145: 2)

Sometimes we're faced with troubles anew
That come so quickly at me and you.
Many times they can knock us off our feet
Leaving us helpless, worn down and beat.
But this is when you must arise
And wipe all tears from your weary eyes.
Believe that God has seen your defeated gaze
And stand to your feet and begin to praise
Him for His goodness, power and grace
Until there's happiness upon your face.
For God desires our praise and inhabits it too,
Only then will He come and comfort you.

In thinking about a final poem to conclude this book that would summarize my reflections of every poem included in **_Reflections_**, the following poem came to mind. I believe that it says it all. I hope that you will agree?

God Still Gets the Glory

The conclusion, when all has been heard, is : fear God and
keep His commandments, because this applies to every
person. (Ecclesiastes 12: 13, <u>New American Standard Bible</u>)

Though the road we travel might be rough and sometimes hard,
Remember, God still gets the glory regardless of where you trod.
Though problems may arise in your life each week…each day,
Remember, God still gets the glory despite what others may say.
Though many times we wonder if God does really care
Because of life's oppression that is seen most everywhere,
Remember, God still gets the glory and our
burdens He willingly does share.
Though oftentimes our backs are pressed against the wall,
Remember, God still gets the glory whether
the situation is large or small.
Though in this life trouble may chain and bound,
Remember, God still gets the glory and can easily be found.
Though we're occasionally bowed beneath a despairing weight,
Remember, God still gets the glory regardless of our fate.
So, just depend on Our God for His mercy and grace
As we live our lives daily in this human race.

Epilogue

Reflections come and reflections go. Some unsettle our minds, others bring peace and comfort. Whatever the effect, they rarely, if ever, evict the exact same emotions on any given day. We may wish that some never come, but that too is a part of life. Perhaps there are some who believe that they can control reflective thoughts, but I seriously doubt it since they tend to come without prior notice. The truth is, we all need our times of reflection. I believe that God has ordained it to be that way. Without these precious moments, we may lose our awareness of just who we are in this very vast universe.

Reflections shape and mold our future. They cause us to go deep within ourselves to look beyond our external environment and seek truths to why we behave in certain ways or why we think the way we do or why we have become who we have become. They can promote suppressed tears and thoughts that may need to surface so that we might live a more wholesome life, with not only ourselves, but with others, as well. They can bring forth much-needed joy, laughter and silliness that we had lost far too long ago. After all, what adult, after having had a carefree childhood, would not want to become as a little child again?

Finally, we all may experience anxiety occasionally, but the Apostle Paul gave us the remedy when it does come. He said, "Be anxious for nothing, but in everything by prayer and supplication, with thanksgiving let your requests be made known to God; and the peace of God, which surpasses, all understanding will guard your hearts and minds through Christ Jesus." (Philippians 4: 6, 7)

He then included how to do so, "Finally, brethren, whatever things are true, whatever things are noble, whatever things are just, whatever things are pure, whatever things are lovely, whatever things are of good report, if there is any virtue and if there is anything praiseworthy, meditate on these things." (Philippians 4: 8)

May the peace of God dwell with you in your moments of reflection!

Bibliography

Kennedy, D. James, *The Real Meaning of the Zodiac* (Coral Ridge Ministries, 1989), 94-96.

Holy Bible: New King James Version Giant Print Center-Column Reference Edition; Thomas Nelson Publishers, Nashville, Tennessee, 1994.

New American Standard Bible; Collins World, The Lockman Foundation 1960, 1962, 1963, 1968, 1971, 1972, 1973, La Habra, California.